4,000

MILES

BY BOOT,

RAFT,

AND SKI

A LONG TREK HOME

Erin McKittrick

THE MOUNTAINEERS BOOKS

is the nonprofit publishing arm of The Mountaineers Club, an organization founded in 1906 and dedicated to the exploration, preservation, and enjoyment of outdoor and wilderness areas.

1001 SW Klickitat Way, Suite 201, Seattle, WA 98134

First edition, 2009
No part of this book may be reproduced in any form,
or by any electronic, mechanical, or other means,
without permission in writing from the publisher.
Distributed in the United Kingdom by Cordee,
www.cordee.co.uk
Manufactured in the United States of America

Copy Editor: Joan Gregory
Cover Design: Mayumi Thompson
Interior Design: Jane Jeszeck, www.jigsawseattle.com
Cartographer: Bretwood Higman
Photographers: Erin McKittrick and Bretwood Higman
Cover photographs: Top: *Erin looks out across the swirling sea ice of Knik Arm.* Bottom: *Hiking the volcanic rock beaches of the Alaska Peninsula in a flash of evening sun*
Frontispiece: *Banks of fog obscure the steep mountains lining the Chikamin River in Alaska's Misty Fiords.*

Library of Congress Cataloging-in-Publication Data
McKittrick, Erin.
  A long trek home : 4000 miles by boot, raft, and ski /
Erin McKittrick. — 1st ed.
      p. cm.
  ISBN 978-1-59485-093-6
  1. Northwest Coast of North America—Description and travel.
2. Hiking—Northwest Coast of North America. 3. Rafting (Sports)—
Northwest Coast of North America. 4. Skiing—Northwest Coast
of North America. 5. McKittrick, Erin—Travel. I. Title.
  F852.3.M39 2009
  979.5—dc22
                                        2009028197

To the Pacific Coast

CONTENTS

WINTER

Map 107

SPRING

Map 171

Alaska

WINTER

BERING
SEA

SPRING

Alaska Peninsula

Seldovia

GULF OF ALA

Unimak Island, June 27, 2008

PACIFI
OCEAN

N

500 miles

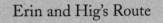

Erin and Hig's Route

ost Coast

FALL

Inside passage

British
Columbia

SUMMER

Seattle
June 9, 2007

Prologue: LEAVING

THE PLAN WAS TO WALK, to paddle, and to ski. To leave Seattle and reach the Aleutian Islands under our own power. To travel not just in summer, but also through an entire Alaskan winter. To travel more than 4,000 miles.

We were about to do something audacious. We were about to do something no one had ever done before. I couldn't grasp the full extent of it any more than could our most skeptical questioners. We planned it, we breathed it, we believed it, but it seemed as though we spent all our time proclaiming a plan that didn't feel real.

...

I picked up a thick loop of aluminum wire from the top of the pile, turning it over in my hand. Should I wait and ask Hig what to do with it? Maybe he'd argue to keep something so useful-looking, but if I recycled it now, he'd never notice. Undecided, I set it aside.

Piles of stuff covered the floor of our living room, our dining room, our bedroom, and our kitchen. More piles of stuff sat on the lawn, along with most of our remaining furniture, decorated with "Free" signs. A few fluffy white feathers drifted around the corners of the dining room, escapees from when we'd sewn a down quilt a few weeks earlier. Colorful scraps of fleece, nylon, webbing, and insulation left over from gear construction were bursting out of a cardboard box.

I glanced up the street, looking hopefully for any sort of delivery truck. We were still waiting on a few crucial pieces of expedition gear. If they didn't come soon, we would have to figure out some way to get them en route. We still needed the packrafts—the five-pound inflatable boats that would ferry us across the many expanses of water we would encounter. We still needed paddles. We still needed dry suits—our only outerwear for the trip. I didn't know how any of these items could possibly catch up with us if they didn't come before we left. But there wasn't much I could do. The invitations were out. We were leaving on Saturday, June 9, 2007, at noon. And that date was now less than a week away.

On computer maps, my husband, Hig, and I had drawn an imaginary line—a bold black stripe across the digital landscape. Beginning at our Seattle doorstep, the line snaked back and forth between the Cascade Range and Puget Sound and then headed north to the Canadian border. From there, our route followed the Inside Passage, weaving through the protected network of inland waterways and forested islands that stretches from Puget Sound through coastal British Columbia and Southeast Alaska. Where the Inside Passage ends, we planned to continue on to the Lost Coast, a narrow strip of surf-battered shore between the Gulf of Alaska and the mountains and glaciers of the St. Elias Range. We would then make our way through Prince William Sound and along the edge of the Chugach Mountains to Anchorage. At Anchorage, our northern-trending route would turn southwest, weaving back and forth between the Pacific Ocean and the Bering Sea, the two coasts of the volcanic Alaska Peninsula. Finally, at the tip of the Alaska Peninsula, we would cross to Unimak Island, the first in the Aleutian chain. Our intricate plan would take us through urban streets, dense rainforests, sandy beaches, glacial rivers, windswept tundra, snowy valleys, protected inlets, wild oceans, and the flanks of volcanoes. Our 4,000-mile journey had been a year in the planning. At the time we left, we expected our trip to take nine months.

· · ·

Hig and I met at a Minnesota college. I had grown up in Seattle; Hig was raised in the tiny Alaskan town of Seldovia. We bonded over our joint love of science—me studying biology while he studied geology. But our relationship was cemented in the Alaskan wilderness.

When I graduated from college, we trekked 800 miles down the Alaska Peninsula. It was the beginning of an addiction. Each summer we were pulled north for a new adventure. In the seven years since that first journey, we had traveled over 3,000 miles through the Alaskan wilderness. And as we journeyed, our dreams grew grander and grander, seeking only the time to be realized. Less than twenty-four hours before we planned to leave, Hig graduated with his PhD in geologic hazards. It was a break in our lives. With no commitments, we had the space to do something truly momentous.

• • •

From the intricate terrain of mountains, ocean, and glaciers, to the abundant wildlife, to the friendly outposts of civilization, the northwest Pacific coast was our favorite place on Earth. And though we had seen only a few small pieces of our proposed 4,000-mile route, we thought of it all as home ground.

This region has a wealth of natural resources: forests, fish, oil, coal, and metals. It has vast stretches of wilderness, vast swaths of industrial development, and vast environmental battlegrounds. On this broad journey, we wanted more than just an amazing adventure. We hoped to get the big picture of what was happening in this region we loved. How could the people living here thrive alongside the natural world around them?

We saw ourselves as explorers. And we gave ourselves one simple rule for the journey: "No Motorized Transport." In order to get the most complete picture of what was going on, we had to experience everything— not just the amazing wild places, but also the clear cuts, suburbs, and noisy urban landscapes on our path. Whether walking, skiing, or paddling, every inch of this journey would be under our own power—viewing the world at human speed.

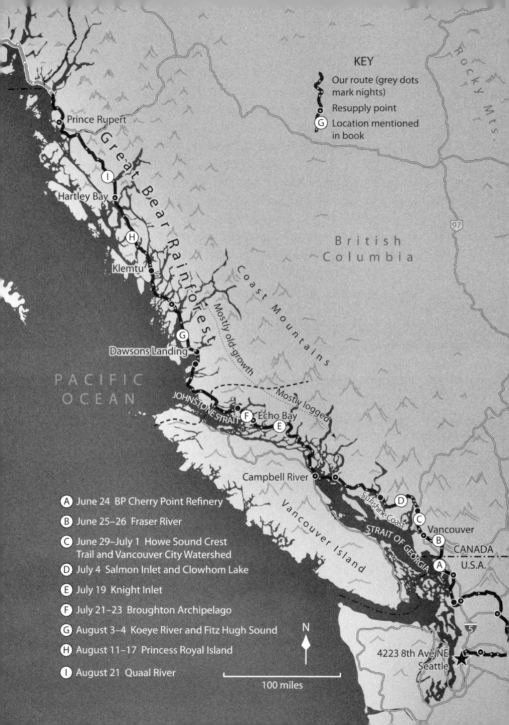

KEY

Our route (grey dots mark nights)

Resupply point

Ⓖ Location mentioned in book

ROCKY Mts.

Prince Rupert

Great Bear Rainforest

Ⓘ

Hartley Bay

Ⓗ

Klemtu

British Columbia

97

Coast Mountains

Ⓖ

Dawsons Landing

Mostly old-growth

Mostly logged

PACIFIC OCEAN

JOHNSTONE STRAIT

Ⓕ

Echo Bay

Ⓔ

Campbell River

Vancouver Island

Sunshine Coast

Ⓓ

STRAIT OF GEORGIA

Ⓒ Vancouver

Ⓑ CANADA

Ⓐ U.S.A.

Ⓐ June 24 BP Cherry Point Refinery

Ⓑ June 25–26 Fraser River

Ⓒ June 29–July 1 Howe Sound Crest Trail and Vancouver City Watershed

Ⓓ July 4 Salmon Inlet and Clowhom Lake

Ⓔ July 19 Knight Inlet

Ⓕ July 21–23 Broughton Archipelago

Ⓖ August 3–4 Koeye River and Fitz Hugh Sound

Ⓗ August 11–17 Princess Royal Island

Ⓘ August 21 Quaal River

N

4223 8th Ave NE Seattle

5

100 miles

SUMMER

[JUNE 9–AUGUST 27]

1,030 MILES

1. CIVILIZATION

Watershed security official:
"Good luck! Thanks for trespassing!"

SLOWLY, PEOPLE BEGAN GATHERING on our front lawn. Enclosed in raincoats or hiding beneath umbrellas, they milled around in the drizzle—friends and family from various corners of our lives. My aunt held a giant banner that read, "Walking to Alaska." My dad and stepmom offered me a freshly baked chocolate chip cookie. We tried to make coherent conversation, but we had nothing to talk about except this trip, and about that there was little left to say. We'd been talking of nothing else for months.

Returning the key to our landlord was the last thing on our list, the last thread tying us to our former lives. I took one final glance around the empty living room, then stepped onto the porch, closed the door, locked it, and dropped the key into my landlord's waiting palm.

. . .

Dressed in matching dry suits, bright-yellow hiking socks, and brand-new trail-running shoes, with ice axes strapped to our backpacks, we stepped onto the sidewalk. I had taken this step every day of the three years we'd lived here. But this time, it wasn't for an hour-long errand run. This time, it was the first step of a 4,000-mile journey. We had made no plans beyond our arrival in the Aleutian Islands. We didn't know if we would ever come back.

The gear in our homemade backpacks spanned the range from homemade, fleece long underwear to expensive camera lenses. Most of what we

Lion's Gate Bridge proves a busy pathway out of the city of Vancouver, British Columbia.

hadn't made ourselves was sponsored by the gear companies that had manufactured it. We purchased some of it through expedition grants, grants from
environmental groups, and generous donations from the folks who knew us.
The whole journey would cost about fifteen thousand dollars. From now on,
nearly all our money would go toward food.

When we started down the street, we had a parade of thirty friends
and family walking with us. Over the next few miles, our entourage slowly
peeled away, as various relatives and friends gave us hugs and farewells
before returning to their cars.

By the end of the afternoon's drizzly twelve-mile walk, only one friend
still accompanied us. We stopped for dinner in a Mexican restaurant, then
said a final farewell and turned off toward a suburban trailer park.

· · ·

Straight north from Seattle was the urban corridor surrounding the
Interstate-5 freeway—exactly where we needed to go, and exactly where we
didn't want to walk. So for the next two weeks, we zigged and zagged our
way toward the Canadian border, bouncing between Puget Sound and the
mountains of the Cascade Range.

We climbed to mountain forests, where row upon row of skinny
cedars and Douglas firs disappeared into the mist, punctuated by the
occasional giant. Each giant old tree stood like a castle, crooked, weather-
beaten, and ancient. The tops of the trees faded into the overhanging fog
until they were indistinguishable from the sky. Water dripped from each
mossy branch. Against the misty grey, the mosses and ferns shone a brilliant and unreal green. It was gorgeous. But eventually, our route would
spit us back onto the roads. To get where we were going, we first had to
escape civilization.

· · ·

Each footfall on the hard asphalt sent a tiny jolt of pain up through the base
of my heels and further reddened the already-sensitive skin at the bottoms
of my feet. In our frenzy of planning, we hadn't trained for this journey at
all. And while my muscles were getting stronger, my feet seemed like they'd
never get broken in. They were only getting broken.

Our thin synthetic shorts and shirts were already stained brown with dust and sweat. On our heads, we wore matching wide-brimmed hats with a white and black camouflage pattern that the tag had called "tundra camo." We'd picked them up for $6.99 in a highway gas station we'd stumbled across one day out of Seattle—a last minute addition to our carefully planned list of gear. Somehow, in planning for an expedition that would bring us through so much cold, rain, and snow, we'd barely stopped to consider the summer sun.

Cars zoomed past, bathing us in the fumes of their exhaust. It was sunny, hot, and boring. We were still in a world of people, not wilderness. And the ironic thing about this crowded world is that the more people there are around, the fewer you actually see.

People surrounded us. They flashed by behind the tinted windows of their cars, or glanced at us from sun-drenched yards. But they moved in their own private bubbles. And although we looked bizarre, with our funny clothes, bulging backpacks, and dangling ice axes, we felt invisible. In journeys through more remote lands, Hig and I talked to nearly everybody we saw. Here, we spoke to no one.

• • •

Wherever we could, we left the roads behind—often avoiding walking altogether. On this journey, we had a secret weapon to get through areas that were unpleasant, impractical, or impossible on foot. We had packrafts.

A packraft is a small inflatable raft, just big enough to hold one person plus one person's gear. Our packrafts are a little over five-and-a-half feet long, weighing just four pounds—five with the spray deck. Deflated, each one packs down into a rubbery yellow roll the size of a tent, fitting nicely into a backpack. Constructed from high-tech urethane-coated fabrics, they look as fragile as pool toys, yet bounce easily off rocks and barnacles. Paired with our two feet, these inflatable wonders allowed us to go more places than any other form of transportation—at a maximum speed of two miles an hour.

Along our wet, coastal route, rushing rivers and miles-wide bays would be common. Swimming with packs in the cold rough water wasn't an option. With packrafts, we could float down glacial rivers, shoot through tidal rapids, paddle stormy coastlines, and hop between islands. And when we packed them up, we could scramble over mountain ridges, walk beaches or roads, bushwhack through the forest, and ski tundra valleys. They were what made this amphibious journey possible.

· · ·

Two weeks into our journey, we ran into a long line of barbed-wire fence walling off the BP Cherry Point oil refinery near Bellingham, Washington. So we pulled out the packrafts, launching into a stiff breeze coming off the water.

Long docks jutted far into the wind-whipped bay, making even the tankers moored at their far ends appear small. It looked so tempting to paddle right between the massive pilings. We headed toward a sign on the dock, its black letters slowly resolving into a warning to stay at least 300 feet away from all docks and oil tankers. By the time we could read it, I was sure we were inside the boundary—already a threat.

We turned to paddle out again. The enormous, blue-metal hull of the tanker dwarfed our tiny yellow rafts. We kept our packrafts pointed out into the choppy waves, trying to keep our distance from the tankers as a side-on wind drove us toward them. High above us on the deck of the ship, toy-sized figures in bright orange raingear moved around, performing their mysterious tasks. I heard a whistle, followed by a yell that was incoherent over the wind and the waves. I waved at the distant man in orange before turning to paddle away again.

How far was 300 feet? We zigzagged our way around a second tanker. Grateful to be beyond the hulking ships at last, we scurried toward the calmer waters near the beach.

It was at least fifteen minutes before the Coast Guard caught up with us. We paddled on blithely, until the trajectory of the zooming red and black Zodiac made it clear that they were after *us*.

"Looks like they want to talk to us," Hig observed.

I took a few nervous paddle strokes forward. "We're not doing anything wrong, are we?"

"Not unless these life vests aren't legal," Hig mused, looking down at the jerry-rigged black and orange life vest on his chest. We'd made them by cutting and resealing inflatable sleeping pads.

"Well, you were inside the 300-foot limit, so it's a security breach, and we have to look inside your bags," said the gruff-looking man holding the clipboard.

I turned to Hig, giving him a frightened "You deal with this!" look as we paddled up to the side of the boat. I hate getting in trouble.

Hig scrambled up over the side of the Coast Guard boat and pulled his packraft after him, flopping it onto the deck. He began unpacking almost gleefully—relishing the ridiculous encounter that had me worried. From dry bags he pulled out our sleeping bag, his smelly socks, food—all the while chatting away about our planned trip. I stayed quiet, one hand clutching the rail of the boat as my packraft thumped into the side with every wave.

Half of their questions were attempts to ferret out any potential terrorist ties, while the other half were directed at ensuring that this pair of potential terrorists wouldn't drown.

"Did you work in Indonesia?" the man with the clipboard asked suspiciously, eyeing the stamp in Hig's passport.

"Do you have an EPIRB [emergency position indicating radio beacon]?" he asked concernedly, eyeing the fragile-looking little raft.

Luckily, it didn't take them long to determine that whatever delusions motivated us to undertake this journey, we posed no risk to an oil tanker. At that point, they morphed from a bunch of intimidating officials to Hig's friendly and interested audience. We hung out for another fifteen minutes, while Hig told stories and shared our plans, passing out business cards with a map of our route on them. They never bothered to look through my pack.

• • •

I slept fitfully, waking in turn to the alternating rackets of hooting tugboats, howling sirens, and cackling crows. The bottom edge of our shelter stood three feet above the ground, perched awkwardly on the tops of salal bushes. We'd pulled out and bent over just enough of the woody stems to give us a space to sleep. Peering out between the sticks and leaves,

I could see just a few glints of twinkling light from the city surrounding us. In the middle of Vancouver, British Columbia, we were invisible.

We were camped on a tiny island in the middle of the Fraser River, guarded from the city by channels of water and a fringe of thorny blackberry bushes at the island's edge. Our shelter was a simple pyramid of silnylon—a slippery, waterproof, and extremely lightweight fabric. It had long strings to serve as ties on each corner and a zipper on one side. In the center, the whole structure was supported by one of our kayak paddles. Around the edges, we tied each corner to a salal bush. In other campsites, we used rocks, logs, or trees—we never carried stakes. Somewhere in the grey area between a tent and a tarp, our eight-by-eight-foot pyramid lacked a floor—so there were nearly as many bushes inside as out. The whole thing weighed about a pound.

One of our packrafts was under our bed, protecting the sleeping pads from stray sticks and punctures. The other was suspended in the bushes, dragged just as far in from the water as we'd been willing to bring it. The way in and out of our tiny campsite was over a long slippery log. To get here, we had to balance on the precarious bridge with all our gear, stepping carefully so as not to fall into the thorny brambles on either side.

During this civilized portion of our journey, we'd been forced to be creative with our campsites. Where we could, we crashed with friends. Occasionally, we took a room for the night in a cheap motel. The rest of the time, we found a spot for our shelter in some nondescript corner of wooded land. Sometimes we were deep in the forest. Other times we camped just far enough from the road to be invisible. Sometimes the land was public, sometimes not, and often—such as here on the Fraser—we didn't even know.

. . .

We'd entered Vancouver on a route usually seen only by tugboat captains, near one of the many log mills lining the banks of the Fraser. Towers of lethal-looking machinery rumbled and clanked beside us as we inflated our boats. Saws buzzed and roared as great contraptions swallowed logs whole, consuming them in a plume of sawdust or belching out great piles of woodchips.

The Fraser carried us on a lazy drift into the heart of the city, accompanied by logs. On every bank, boom chains linked the outermost logs end to end, corralling the rows of fresh timber. Bright identifying marks tagged the end of each cut log. We picked out spruce, Douglas fir, and red cedar, musing over other conifers we couldn't identify in log form. A few of the trees looked like ancient giants, but most of the logs had the lanky spindly look of second- or third-growth adolescents.

Ahead of us, tugboats maneuvered a long raft of logs, towing them upriver to one of the chip mills. Behind us, another set of tugs pulled a barge full of wood chips back down. Somewhere on the British Columbia coast, acres of trees were falling to the chainsaws. I wondered what awaited us in the forests.

• • •

Barely beyond the city's edge, we entered the British Columbia Coast Mountains and headed north on the Howe Sound Crest Trail. It was meant to be a quick escape. For a trail so close to so many people, I was expecting a tame and well-trodden footpath. Instead, we soon found ourselves in a painstakingly creeping traverse along slippery ground, on the edge of an infinite drop, high above a route that was buried in twelve feet of snow.

Wet flakes sprayed into my eyes as Hig swung his ice ax, cutting a ladder of steps in the snow above me. After three or four of these steep traverses, my vertigo was getting the better of me. With each step, the slope seemed steeper, the snow slipperier, and the steps Hig was cutting ever more shallow.

"No more mountains!" I yelled, only half-joking. "Not for at least another month—until all this snow melts!"

Hig's ankles were getting tired. My vertigo was getting worse. Finally, we decided to head down—along one of the few cliff-less gaps to the valley below.

In the base of the valley, we walked a gravel road under a hot and climbing sun. The cold snow and towering heights of the Howe Sound Crest Trail were obscured behind the thick trees on the slope. After our painstaking traverse on the ridge, the mindless progression of smooth gravel was refreshing.

A white truck with the words "Greater Vancouver Regional District" painted prominently on its side pulled up beside us. A man leaned his head out the window, and in a strong Swedish accent asked, "Are you lost?"

"No," I replied with a greater air of confidence than I really felt. Things were suddenly clicking: The absence of recent logging on such a well-maintained road, the tidy and well-labeled stream crossings, the absence of any vehicles other than this white truck, the official logo on this white truck....

Hig jumped in. "We've just come down from the Crest Trail," he explained, gesturing up toward the peaks. "And now we're headed out to Howe Sound."

The man frowned at us slightly. "Well, you're trespassing right now. You're inside a restricted area."

"I'm sorry," I said helplessly. "We didn't know. And we didn't see any signs," I added with a nervous defiance.

"It's OK," he reassured me. "No big deal, but I do have to take down your names and addresses."

He introduced himself as Conny, and as we dug for our passports in the depths of a dry bag, he explained that we were in the watershed that provided drinking water to the city of Vancouver.

When I get in trouble with officials, I expect them to be stern and forbidding. Conny, however, seemed extremely excited to have trespassers. Perhaps driving circles on empty logging roads all day isn't the most exciting of occupations.

"Can I give you a ride?" Conny asked, after all the formalities were completed.

We tried to weasel out of it. We tried to play off the excitement we'd generated about our trip. We pleaded that we had *only one rule—no motorized transport!* We promised to scurry along on foot straight out of the restricted area.

Conny thought about it for a second, but then firmly refused. He said he had no authority to make exceptions. I reluctantly threw my pack into the back of the truck, climbed in, and we zipped five miles over the dusty gravel to a locked fence.

He handed us his business card as we hopped out of the truck. "Good luck! Thanks for trespassing!"

I grumbled as we headed down the public road, frustrated at being forced to break our one rule so early in the trip. Hig took it in stride.

"OK, so it's 'no motorized transport' with one condition—'except by force of authority'. That doesn't really detract from anything. And besides, it's a cool story. Running into Conny was interesting," he argued.

It was interesting, but I refused to be convinced out of my sullenness.

I felt as though the journey so far had been laced in a web of human rules and restrictions that we'd been alternately weaving our way around or running headlong into. I couldn't wait to hit the wilderness.

2. SEEKING FORESTS

Spray-painted boulder on the side of the road:
"10 minutes to HELL."

ON THE FAR SIDE of Howe Sound, we followed another set of gravel roads where we weren't supposed to be, climbing up the valley past a shutdown pulp mill. Then we left the roads behind to walk through a forest of stick-straight, spindly, and nearly identical hemlocks, each with the diameter of a dinner plate. The dark forest floor was nearly devoid of undergrowth, and as we sped through it, we marveled at the huge old cedar stumps interspersed among the younger trees, the stumps easily ten or twenty times the size of their younger kin.

Each stump bore narrow horizontal slits where loggers of a past generation had stood on springboards, using their long saws to send the big trees toppling. The slits stared at us from mossy knobbed faces of weathered wood. It felt as though the eyes of ghosts were watching us.

Blinking and squinting, we left the dim shelter of the forest for the glaring brightness of a fresh clear cut. The scent of newly cut wood wafted over us. Skinny hemlock trunks littered the ground in a half-finished game of pick-up sticks. We balanced on the long and slender logs, using them as bridges to cross the treacherous slash of stumps and branches between the edge of the clear cut and another logging road. The logging area was silent today, the machines abandoned next to stacks of long thin logs. No one

Stump on a stump: A fresh clear cut of second-growth trees reveals giant cedar stumps from the original forest in British Columbia's Great Bear Rainforest.

was the wiser as we passed through to the older and uninhabited lands of washed-out logging roads, then up into the fog, rock, and snow.

. . .

The mountains called to us. Our route wound up, down, and over the steep and convoluted mountains that separate the equally convoluted fiords of southern British Columbia. Despite our difficulties on the Howe Sound Crest Trail, we climbed again.

From the top, I peered over the edge. When we'd looked at the map, Hig had called it a "tight spot." In reality, it was a cliff.

"What does it look like?" I yelled down to Hig, invisible below me as he scouted a possible route.

"Well, I think there's a way…," he began cautiously. "I didn't go all the way out there, but there's a stone ledge that doesn't look too hard to crawl out onto, and I think it might be OK from there. The ledge is wide enough, but there is a drop off beyond it…" He trailed off.

I pressed him for details and he described an extremely narrow shelf, slanting down toward the hundred-foot drop beneath it. It offered barely enough room for a person plus backpack and only a few little alder branches to serve as handholds.

"I am *not* crawling out along that ledge—and definitely not over that drop off," I said emphatically. "We'll just have to find another way."

"Well… I'll look over at the gully there, but I don't think it will work."

It was Hig's turn to lead our expedition. We made most major route decisions by consensus. But for the smaller decisions, we found it worked best if one of us was the official "leader." Every few days, we handed off the map, leaving the leader to decide moment-to-moment details of navigation. Always our optimist, Hig had estimated an hour or so to find our way through this "tight spot." He'd already burned at least half that in the scouting.

At one point, the cliff band formed a sharp inside corner. The corner was filled with icy snow clinging to the sixty-degree slope—too steep to descend, even with our ice axes. But underneath that snow was a tunnel melted out by water and air flowing down the cliff. It was just big enough for us to squeeze into.

I wiggled into the muddy hole. The snow above me glowed an eerie light blue, melting and pitted. Icy dribbles and dollops of mud spattered from the roof, pelting my hood. Hig was below me, sending ice chips flying as he swung his ice ax to widen a tiny hole. I passed my backpack to him before slithering down a rocky mudslide, pressed against the cliff by the ice overhead.

"We're not done yet…there's another drop, but I think we can stay under the edge of the snow and do it. I'll cut some steps." Hig was clinging to a thin alder branch decorated with green buds, only recently melted out of the snow. His head was silhouetted against the valley a thousand feet below, peering down to difficulties I couldn't yet see. "I don't think it will be too bad."

Even though he was currently leading, we'd both conspired to land ourselves on this cliff. On the one hand, my role in our adventures is to be the big dreamer—always pushing us to do something just a little grander and more amazing. It was I who thought our first journey, down the Alaska Peninsula, should be a full two months, and it was I who convinced Hig that a multi-season trek to the Aleutian Islands was a good idea. On the other hand, my role is to be the "Voice of Reason"—injecting caution, prudence, and a dose of pessimism into every individual route decision. We were trying to descend right here because I'd argued against following the spine of our steep granite ridge in the thick fog.

I wiped my eyes with a muddy hand. Hig was cutting a foothold, wedging himself into the gap where the ice had melted out from the cliff. I sighed as I saw the distance we still had to descend. I could see steep snow interrupted by bits of rock and avalanche-scarred trees. I knew the sections we couldn't see were steeper still. It was enough to make me wish for the logging roads.

. . .

The next morning, safely off the ridge, we got our logging road. Initially overgrown with alder and salmonberry, it joined up with bigger roads at every turn, soon transforming itself into a wide path of dusty gravel bearing tracks of recent use. On the opposite wall of the valley, swaths of fresh clear cut were outlined by roaring waterfalls. Snowy peaks glistened in the sun. In most of the valley, it seemed the loggers were busy downing second-growth trees, while a few braver souls tumbled the last old-growth giants on high steep slopes near the peaks.

Descending through the valley on winding roads, we hit the shores of a long inlet branching off the even longer Sechelt Inlet. There we met Len, joining him as he looked out over the calm, turquoise water from the porch of his fishing lodge.

"This used to be called Salmon Inlet," Len remarked, leaning over the rail. "And the guy who lived here before me—the caretaker—said you could see the salmon running here, right past the dock."

On our map, it was still labeled "Salmon Inlet." But in the 1950s, BC Hydro had dammed the short stretch of river that connected Clowhom Lake to Salmon Inlet, preventing the salmon from returning to spawn and killing off the run. Earlier that day, we'd paddled down the lake, drifting over the stumps of trees that had once grown on its shore. We'd scrambled over the lichen-encrusted rock where the old waterfall had once gushed, a few hundred yards from the river's new course through a hulking concrete power plant. Len told us that money had been set aside for a fish ladder, but the implementation was tied up in a legal argument. Either way, the salmon run was long gone.

The next morning, we watched as the small creeks tumbling into the inlet created sparkling rainbows in the early light. Their waterfalls were too steep, too high, and too small for salmon to leap through. The dammed Clowhom River appeared to be the only stream along Salmon Inlet where wild salmon might once have swum. Now, the only salmon here were in the fish farms—caged Atlantic transplants circling in their pens. The stench of these salmon farms wafted over the inlet, emanating from large plastic tubs labeled "offal."

Every hillside had that close-cropped, too-even look of a sheared forest, with patches of more recent shearing atop the old. Power lines cut across the land and stretched over the water, bringing power from the dam to civilization, somewhere beyond the horizon. There wasn't a house in sight. We'd left the urban world behind. But we weren't in the wilderness.

. . .

We were on the Sunshine Coast. Sliced by deep fjords, this section of British Columbia's mainland sits in the rain shadow of Vancouver Island, drawing tourists to its gleaming waters and sunny skies.

Here in the narrow channels between granite knobs, rushing currents bring a wealth of plankton past every rock, feeding barnacles, anemones, and sea cucumbers, which feed the sea stars and the scuttling crabs. Kelp forests trail their ribbons in the current, teeming with schools of tiny fish. Squawking seagulls and stately looking herons perch on every rock, keeping an eye out for easy prey. Harbor seals splash in the riffles, diving for their dinners in the wealth of life beneath the surface.

On one clear dark night, we paddled under the shining stars of the Milky Way, our packrafts skating along on a glowing cushion of phosphorescence. Each stroke of our paddle blades startled a school of tiny fish. Each fish zipped off in a different direction, followed by its own cloud of phosphorescent sparkles. The water beneath our boats was a starburst of fireworks.

. . .

Along the eastern edge of the Strait of Georgia, we passed through busy towns catering to summer tourists. Deep in the fiords and high on the hillsides, we saw almost no one. But everywhere we went, we found logging camps and fish farms, power lines and dams.

We pounded our feet on winding gravel logging road after winding gravel logging road. Crossing through clear cuts between them, we picked our way carefully through treacherous piles of cut branches and shattered trees that the loggers had left behind, obscured by thorny blackberry vines and the remains of last year's bracken ferns. Ancient crumbling stumps poked out of fireweed meadows, dwarfing the small fresh stumps of the second growth the loggers were cutting. High in the mountains, fresh signs of logging marked cliffs so steep I doubted we could scramble them with our current gear, much less lugging forty-two-inch chainsaws and felling trees. In nearly every lake we paddled, tall snags stood like pillars around the shore, assuring us that the outlet was dammed. Nearly every inlet was dotted with the netted pens of salmon farms. And though we rarely saw people when we ventured into the forests, we never saw a forest people hadn't already logged. With the developers gone, the development seemed strangely lonely. We called it the Industrial Wilderness.

What did I know about British Columbia, anyway? If I'd thought about it, I would have remembered tidbits from my past research—tidbits that would tell me that most of the southern B.C. coast had been logged, that fish farms were common, and that BC Hydro had dammed many of the rivers. I had seen the maps that colored nearly all of the land here in a mottled red or yellow that represented clear cuts. Over 75 percent of this area's old-growth forests has been logged. If you exclude the cliffs too steep to walk, the numbers are even higher. But I hadn't thought about it. I hadn't been prepared for what those numbers would really look like. At least for the moment, we gave up on the land, and returned to the sea.

· · ·

On our seven-mile crossing of the Strait of Georgia near Campbell River, we paused for a break, letting the packrafts spin as we watched the perfectly clear cloud reflections running across the glassy water. It was ninety degrees Fahrenheit under the bright July sun, and even on the water, it was hot. I splashed salty water on my head, trying to keep cool. I wriggled my legs, trying to uncramp them. Usually we didn't go so long without a break on shore.

Every day that we paddled, our transition from land to water got a few minutes faster. Hig usually began with the inflation bag, screwing the plastic nozzle of the thin nylon sack into the valve of his raft. He filled the bag with air, repeatedly, squeezing it into the boat with a rhythmic motion. Meanwhile, I carefully rinsed the sand from each section of my five-piece kayak paddle, snapping and clamping it together. I buckled on my sleeping-pad life vest. Then we switched off.

The rest of the gear went back into the packs, buckled onto the spray decks at the front of each raft. Cinched around our waists, the spray decks kept most of the water from waves, rain, and paddle drips off our laps. But in this heat, we didn't need it. A string ran from the boat, through a loop in the pack, to a loop around the paddle, and finally to a loop around my wrist.

In a river, this much string would put us at risk of tangling with a rock or log. But in the middle of open water, the string was our safety line—no matter what happened, we wouldn't lose our boats.

I'd been on kayak journeys before. Our packrafts were slower and less graceful, but simpler. Instead of cutting smoothly through the water, they wiggled back and forth with each stroke of the paddle. Left to their own devices, the rafts spun in circles. But even laden with all our gear, each raft could easily be lifted with a single hand, to be set down in the water from a perch on a rocky cliff or carried over a field of barnacle-encrusted boulders. To get in, we simply stepped into the boats from the rocks above them, keeping our feet dry in our trail-running shoes. In this land of steep and rocky fiords, we were happy to be able to launch or land anywhere.

• • •

We wove through the maze of islands between Vancouver Island and the mainland, paddling channels and inlets and making short land crossings over low hills and valleys. If we stuck to the packrafts, we could make twenty miles in a day—more with the help of tidal currents. On land, we might cruise even faster along logging roads or through the nearly lifeless understory of newly grown forests. But in the thick and thorny brush of clear cuts, we were lucky to make a quarter of that distance. A mile-long trek through clear cut might take half the day.

It had been over a month since we had left Seattle, and the berry bushes were now at the height of their summer glory. Ripe juicy thimbleberries and blackberries dangled over every logging road and it was only with difficulty that I restrained myself from spending all day picking them. A purple swath of fireweed decorated a newly logged patch with a burst of color, where we marveled at the tiny stump of a freshly cut hemlock. It was perched several feet above our heads, on the giant stump of an ancient cedar. A stump on a stump—new logging on the old. There was probably less wood in that entire tiny hemlock than in the cedar stump left behind.

Theoretically, the forests that once grew could grow again. But here it seemed they never would. The rate of logging vastly outpaced the rate of growth. If the clear-cutting didn't slow down, the race for more wood to fuel the Fraser River chip mills could never be sustained. Compared to a hundred years ago, we were harvesting twigs. A farmland of skinny young trees was supplanting the complex rainforest ecosystem that had once supported the region's wildlife. There would never be thousand-year-old cedars here again.

But even in the midst of this twice-logged area, one huge tree remained. It towered just off an overgrown road, a giant among the toothpick adolescents that suddenly looked small and sickly all around it. Eight feet above the soft dirt floor, the red cedar's trunk split into a many-headed hydra, each trunk four feet in diameter, each winding its separate way to the sky. Scattered around its base, rusting bits of machinery, discarded clamshells, and broken glass told us that we weren't the first to visit this giant. We almost ran toward it in our excitement. It had been nearly two weeks since we had seen our last *living* big old tree—in the restricted area of the Vancouver city watershed. Hig immediately dropped his pack and started climbing, soon peering down from forty feet in the air. I dragged out the camera, ignoring the clouds of mosquitoes biting my hands as I tried to hold it steady in the dim light.

Why was this one tree left behind? Maybe it was the splitting trunks—which would have made it dangerous to cut down and difficult to mill. Or maybe the loggers who'd cut this stretch of forest saw the tree as we did—an amazing giant that ought to stand. I like to think that was at least part of the story.

. . .

Hills of mist obscured the mountains, breaking into stripes, into wisps, and then disappearing as new clouds formed elsewhere. Rain squalls moved around the bay, spattering us when we brushed their edges and dumping great torrents when they passed overhead. Heavy drops pounded on my hood, pooled on my spray deck, and textured the gentle waves with a million tiny drops and ripples. Occasional sunspots made the wet world shine. A rainbow touched down on the far side of Knight Inlet. We paddled over twenty miles along this long straight fjord, just south of the Broughton Archipelago. Every stream was running high in this late July storm, spewing chocolate water with the scent of forest floor into the inlet. And in the distance, porpoises leapt into the air.

Three porpoise-lengths out of the water, flipping and spinning—they were performing in a way I previously thought required a Sea World trainer tossing them fish for inspiration. We watched them leap and spin and swim and dive, slowly moving farther and farther away from us.

"Porpoises sometimes visit boats," I said wistfully as they retreated.

"Maybe if we make some noise?" Hig suggested, rubbing the soles of his shoes back and forth along the rubberized tubes of the raft, making a bizarre series of squeaking and squealing sounds.

I joined in, but the porpoises didn't miss a flip. "At our speed and size, I bet we're about as interesting to them as a pair of floating logs."

The porpoises disappeared beneath the water, a quarter mile away.

"Whoa!" A second before, I'd been paddling across a long straight stretch of smooth opaque water. Suddenly, a sleek grey head and dorsal fin sheared the water. The porpoise had surfaced just in front of my bow—not two feet away—clearly playing with me, cutting as close as only a quick and graceful swimmer could do.

"That was two feet from my boat!" I yelled to Hig.

"I saw the splash!"

Three more porpoises surfaced between our rafts, not ten feet away. If I was anywhere near as fast as a porpoise, I could have touched one with my paddle. I couldn't see the sun, but our rainy world seemed transformed. I felt graced by the visit.

• • •

Wet and bedraggled, we pulled our packrafts onto the end of a float at the Echo Bay Resort on Gilford Island—part of the Broughton Archipelago. I had just dumped the rainwater that had accumulated in my boat when a head poked out of the nearest yacht.

"Would you like a cup of hot tea?"

Dripping, we stepped into the clean, warm yacht, and were immediately offered a dry towel, a wipe for Hig's glasses, and a hot cup of tea. We plugged our various electronic rechargers into the outlets on the yacht and spent the rest of the evening eating and chatting with our hosts. Despite the rain, it seemed an auspicious moment.

We hoped the Broughton Archipelago might be a turning point in our journey. We were getting farther and farther north, closer to our hazy memories of where maps of British Columbia logging had shown some swaths of uncut green. Back home an old family friend had waxed nostalgic about her year as a teacher on Broughton Island. Her reminiscences conjured an image of a remote homestead paradise, and we'd been eager to reach it ever since.

But before we set out for Broughton Island itself, all the tourists at Echo Bay told us we had to visit Billy Proctor. In his over eighty years living in the area, he'd come to know it like no one else. Nearly every boat passing through had copies of his books. We paddled our packrafts to the dock at the head of the bay—the only way to get around in a town that charmingly lacked any land-based streets.

We found Billy Proctor in his museum, a white-haired man surrounded by shelves of glass bottles, ancient artifacts, and other beach-combed treasures.

After a brief introduction, Hig started in, "We've heard you're involved with fighting the fish farms."

"Not anymore," Billy replied gruffly. "I gave up on that."

"Oh," Hig replied, somewhat stumped.

"We have a terrible government," Billy continued.

Over the course of a half hour's conversation, Billy regaled us with a depressing litany: the government permitting more salmon farms despite local protests, clear-cutting right to the banks of salmon streams, herbicides sprayed on logged areas to kill off brush and "release" the conifers, no money for hatcheries to restore the runs, lack of adequate sport-fishing closures, and how a place up the bay he'd been trying to protect for years and years was about to be logged.

"There's hardly anything left around here," he finished.

· · ·

On Broughton Island, we did find a patch of uncut trees. In some ways, this old-growth forest seemed like an ugly mess next to the young forests we'd been traveling through. Trees protruded from a heinously thick salal thicket—tangling my feet and obscuring the treacherous floor of old cedar logs that had lain for centuries without rotting. Snaggy, unkempt-looking cedars, broken-topped and bedecked with witches' hair, towered over the salal. The poorly drained soil was pockmarked with small ponds, breeding the mosquitoes that fed eagerly on our exposed skin.

But thick wild places like this are beautiful in the same way the tangled alleyways of ancient cities are beautiful—they have a sense of unexplored mystery. The profusion and diversity of undergrowth that snagged our feet contrasted with the lifeless dirt floors beneath skinny second-growth trees. And it was unpredictable in a way that only a wild place can be.

The undergrowth was nearly as thick as in the clear cuts, and nearly as frustrating to walk through. But after waiting so long for any sort of uncut forest, I didn't care. I peered around at the wondrous mess, looking for that perfect photo.

Boom! We froze, startled by what sounded like thunder. When the echo of the crash faded, a faint buzzing filtered through the trees, and I half jumped, expecting to find I'd stumbled into a beehive.

"That's a chainsaw, alright," Hig said, noticing my puzzled look. Raised in the city, I'd never learned that distinctive sound.

We never saw the loggers, but the buzz of saws and the frequent tearing crash of trees falling followed us onto the fresh logging roads. We could only speculate that the boom had been dynamiting in a gravel quarry. The mysterious labeling of a boulder perched on the road's edge seemed appropriate: "10 minutes to HELL."

3. PARADISE LONELY

Yacht landing owner: "The only people who walk around here are the logging engineers, and they always carry a sidearm."

I LEANED AGAINST the cedar trunk, one hand feeling the rough fibrous texture of its bark. My face cracked into a grin, and I struggled to hold the expression still but not too robot-like as Hig snapped my picture in the dim light beneath the forest canopy.

We'd treated the first few big trees like long-lost relatives, acting like literal tree-huggers in our excitement to lay our hands on the bark of these giants, craning our necks backwards in awe at their magnificent height. At each one, we rushed to snap a picture, one of us grinning in front of the impressive monument, adding to a steadily growing catalog of "me-and-a-tree" shots. We were approaching the Koeye River, seventy-five miles northwest of Broughton Island, near the shores of Fitz Hugh Sound. By this point in the journey, we expected to see the forests. But my mind was still full of the images of stumps, and I wasn't ready to take these giants for granted.

It wasn't a political boundary. It wasn't even a protected area boundary. But somewhere between southern and northern British Columbia, two months from our journey's beginning, we had crossed an invisible line. We had entered the forests.

The Great Bear Rainforest spans the northern half of coastal British Columbia, from Johnstone Strait to the border with Alaska. It's a name

Our packrafts pass beneath the boughs of overhanging trees on the shores of Fish Egg Inlet, in the Great Bear Rainforest.

applied to a 25,000-square-mile region, part of the temperate rainforest ecosystem that once stretched from northern California to Southcentral Alaska. To the south, most of the forest has already been logged. To the north, the increasingly harsh climate limits where forests can grow. As a result, the Great Bear contains the largest area of uncut temperate rainforest in the world.

Not that this northern land was untouched wilderness. We never noticed the arbitrary boundary that marks the beginning of the Great Bear Rainforest, drawn across a continuum of deep fjords and scattered islands in the heart of logging country. It wasn't until we were beyond the northern end of Vancouver Island that slowly, old-growth patch by old-growth patch, the forests began to appear.

Deep in remote groves, we still stumbled across trailing orange streamers of flagging tape, the words "Falling Boundary" printed in block capital letters on each one. Beyond the streamers, we found prize patches of giant red cedars freshly razed to the ground. There was other logging and other development.

But still. There were forests.

. . .

A few days earlier, we had paddled up to Dawsons Landing on Rivers Inlet, one of many floating outposts on the B.C. coast providing traveling boaters with food, showers, laundry, and lodging. Talking to the storeowner, Hig fished for local info about the next section of our route.

"Does anyone ever walk up over the ridge here?" he asked casually.

"No," the woman replied vehemently, taken aback. "No. The only people who walk around here are the logging engineers, and they always carry a sidearm."

She looked at us as though we were more than a little crazy. "There was one woman, back when my husband was a kid, who used to walk up and down the inlet sometimes. But she died. They found her body in the woods back here after she'd been missing about a month."

Despite the fact that it was a "scary thought," she did give us permission to cross her land on our way over the ridge. We followed a boardwalk trail a short distance to the tiny dam her family used to create their water supply. Beyond the dam, all signs of people disappeared. We were walking on a carpet of needles, beneath the cool shade of Sitka spruce and red and yellow cedar. It might have been miles from anywhere.

Despite all the boaters plying the inlets and bays, the forested islands sprinkling these smooth waterways might as well be the darkest heart of the Amazon. All the way from the logged-over south to the more pristine north, no one except the loggers ventures into the forest. It remains a dark and shadowy mystery.

. . .

Even in the rain, the bark on the trunks felt dry beneath the moss. My feet squelched into the sphagnum, each step making a sticky *shluuuck* sound as the mud grabbed the sole of my shoe. Beyond the edge of the meadow, the wet skunk cabbage leaves broke underfoot with a squeaky crunch. Stubby cedar branches whacked my shins, catching on the legs of my dry suit. I pulled a rain-sparkling blueberry bush toward my face, plucking a berry with my teeth as the sopping branches gently slapped my nose.

Hig says that bushwhacking can be graceful.

I stepped onto a mossy log, balancing carefully, my quick, sure steps carrying me along the narrow bridge over thick undergrowth on the forest floor. I wove through blueberry bushes until a larger log blocked my path. I grabbed onto the stub of a decaying branch with one hand and pulled myself easily up and over the obstacle, with arms newly muscled from a month of paddling. At the next log, I dropped to my knees on the wet sphagnum floor, swinging sideways to get my pack underneath.

Backpacks are the curse of backpackers. If we carried nothing, we could be light and agile on our feet. But we would also be spending all our time simply trying to survive—building shelters of sticks and moss, improvising snares and fishing tackle, doing anything we could simply to eat and keep warm. So to fend off the elements, Hig and I carried a shelter, sleeping pads, a sleeping bag, a fleece suit, and a dry suit. We carried matches and lighters, a pot for cooking hot meals, a tiny wood-burning stove, and bottles for water. We carried cameras and batteries and a waterproof journal. We carried the packrafts and paddles that had allowed us to reach the island we stood on. We even carried an EPIRB—a satellite locator beacon—to call the Coast Guard in case of an emergency we couldn't wriggle out of on our own. And all of this stuff was carefully sealed into waterproof bags and shoved into a pair of overfull packs.

We went as light as we could. Every grubby item in our packs was the result of an agonizing and calculated choice—its weight plotted on spreadsheets, its value carefully examined. We jettisoned hiking boots for lighter trail-running shoes that dealt well with water. We carried just enough clothing to keep us warm in the coldest conditions—no spares. Our "house" was a simple, one-pound pyramid shelter. We did lug five pounds worth of camera equipment, but great pictures weren't something we were willing to give up. Without food or water, our packs weighed roughly twenty pounds each. With the food we'd acquired at Dawsons Landing, they were probably closer to thirty.

Each ounce we carried made our trip more possible, more enjoyable, more comfortable—safer. And each ounce we carried made our trip less possible, less enjoyable, less comfortable—less safe. The more we added to our packs, the less sure we were of each step we took. Each mile was more toil. Each day ended in less distance covered.

We couldn't do without our backpacks. I only wished they were smaller. I pulled my pack through a gap between branches, managing to avoid being stuck. It felt smooth and agile. I almost started to agree with Hig about the gracefulness of bushwhacking. Then the ground disappeared beneath me. One step onto a tuft of bright green moss suspended over nothing, and I fell upside down, head-over-heels, contemplating the slightly musky smell of the damp forest floor, now mere inches from my nose.

• • •

The sky was hung with glittering white stars, slowly turning from a deep, velvety black to indigo blue with the approaching dawn. On this clear summer night, we hadn't even bothered with our shelter.

It was 4:30 in the morning—still dark. With unreasonable enthusiasm for such an early hour, Hig propelled himself out of our sleeping bag, planted his hand on a nearby log, and promptly snapped the arm off the glasses he'd left there the night before. This little accident, compounded by further wrongs against his glasses, would leave Hig half-blind by the end of the trip. I opened my eyes, peered blearily at the gorgeous skies, then grumpily pulled the covers over my head again.

The sharp crack of breaking sticks broke the silence on our starry beach. Hig was filling our tiny wood stove with dead branches and bits of driftwood, heating water for coffee. I sat up in the sleeping bag, slowly stuffing gear into dry bags, putting off as long as possible the moment when I would finally have to emerge from my warm cocoon.

We had vowed to awaken at this unreasonable hour because the previous day we had stopped long before sunset. We had stopped because we were paddling into the glaring reflection of the western sun and a stiff and increasing breeze on Seaforth Channel, roughly at the midpoint of the Great Bear Rainforest. Today, we wanted an early start, so we could make some headway before the wind came up again. I tried to remind myself of that practicality as I stumbled groggily through the dark.

The deep-blue sky slowly turned pink behind us as we launched the rafts at 5:30. Soon a warm golden sun was pursuing us, tinting the world a fiery orange, highlighting the rough textures of the granite cliffs, and penetrating the shadows of the cool morning. With the dropping of the tide, we journeyed through a completely different world from what we'd seen at high tide the night before. Gooey pink anemones hung on the rocks like drooping blobs of slime, tentacles tucked in against the dryness of the open air. The rocks they clung to were painted an even brighter shade of magenta-pink by the coralline algae that encrusted their surfaces. A bright red blood star hid shyly behind the seaweed, two of its legs barely visible behind a ruffled and slippery brown frond. Red and purple sea urchins hung at the intersection of water and air, waving their spines as the swell washed over them.

"Sea urchins are edible, right?" Hig asked as we watched them.

But while we were certain they were, neither of us had any clue how to prepare them, or even which part we were supposed to eat. We settled for cookies.

...

Three days later, we reached Princess Royal Island, in the heart of the Great Bear Rainforest. From its hilltops, we could see across the island and to islands beyond. It was an infinity of lush green and turquoise blue. Green ridges rose from winding green valleys. Pools of turquoise lakes blended into lagoons that blended into deep-blue saltwater inlets. Half forest, half water—the world was half-submerged. Thousands of years ago, ice age glaciers had sculpted the hills and valleys from granite. As the glaciers retreated, the water from all that melted ice raised the ocean levels—flooding the valleys into a world of fjords and islands.

The hard granite edges of Princess Royal Island leave no beaches to separate water and land. Lush forests reach down to nearly kiss the sea, and the highest tides drape kelp on the drooping limbs of red and yellow cedars. As we paddled along the mirror-smooth water, reflected forests reached up from the depths, curved limbs of cedars straining to touch the sky.

The island is best known for its snow-white "Kermode" or "spirit" bears—a rare variant of the black bear found only in this area. Over the years, Hig and I had traveled thousands of miles through bear country and had seen hundreds of bears, both black and brown. But a white one—that would be something special.

Every time we came around a corner—a bend in a bear trail or a small nook along the shoreline of a lake or inlet—I'd tell Hig, "Sssshhh...!"

We would gentle our footsteps or dip the paddle blades more smoothly and soundlessly, keeping our eyes peeled for a flash of white fur, the movement of a bush...but no luck. The white giants eluded us. By walking in their trails, however—stepping in their tracks and sidestepping piles of their scat—we knew we were in their world.

...

The tide was dropping. Mist rose from the water of Laredo Inlet as the sun began to light the mountains of Princess Royal Island. Splashes rippled the smooth water where a creek poured into the inlet—salmon schooling and leaping as they waited to swim upstream. I swung the lens of the camera back and forth, missing the jumpers by fractions of a second, frozen hands clenched around the camera in the chill morning air.

We turned our backs on the inlet, following the creek upstream. Giant Sitka spruce lined its banks, draped in garlands of yellow-green moss. As the warm August sun rose over the land, we splashed right into the stream, enjoying the cool flow of the water around our ankles, knees, and sometimes thighs.

A green film of algae coated the smooth grey gravel in the stiller pools. Tall forests blocked the sea breeze. The air hung still and hot. Flies buzzed around us, exploring every inch of our skin to find the tastiest place to bite. The red welts they left behind added to the lacework of red scratches left by the twisted and dwarfed yellow cedars in the marshes. The high-pitched whine of the smaller insects was shot through with the deeper ominous drone of the horsefly.

"When I kill the little flies," Hig commented, pinching the carcass of a horsefly between his thumb and forefinger, "it's just mashing a little bit of parasite paste into my skin. But when I kill a horsefly? That's doing battle."

He dropped the dead fly into the stream. The bent-winged body bobbed on the surface, drifting with the gentle current. And with a sudden jerk, it was gone.

A spotted salmon fry was streaking under the water, the horsefly only half engulfed by its too-small mouth, sprinting for all that it was worth to outdistance the hungry pack behind it. Another fry pulled ahead, snatching the half of the horsefly still protruding, wresting the whole thing away. A great struggle ensued, as salmon after salmon, tearing off wings, legs, and chunks of meat in the process, grabbed the horsefly until finally it was small enough that the one lucky fry swallowed it whole.

Hig and I had crept out to the end of a log suspended over a pool in the stream. We bent low over the water, watching the spectacle, speaking in whispers to avoid scaring the young salmon. After the fry's last gulp, we immediately turned our heads to the sound of the nearest deep buzzing, looking for more horseflies to fuel this miniscule gladiatorial spectacle.

. . .

In alpine meadows above the edge of Princess Royal's forests, we walked in the unshaded realm of granite knobs, lupine fields, and three-foot-tall twisted trees. The sun beat down. We filled our goofy camouflage sun hats with snow from a tiny remnant patch tucked into a gully, my fingers turning raw as they scraped at the icy crust. I packed so much into my over-large hat that I felt top heavy, like one of those bobbing head dolls. Rivulets of melting snow ran down my neck and face, stinging my eyes as the cool water picked up the dried crust of salty sweat from my forehead.

At the edge of an alpine lake, I perched on a granite ledge, wriggling my toes in the ice-cold water as I looked out into the turquoise depths.

I turned toward Hig, who was standing high and dry with camera in hand. "Are you ready?"

"Well, if you're going to do it," he said dubiously, "I probably will too. But I'll take a picture first and see how bad it is before I decide."

"Wuss!" I laughed at him, jumping off the ledge with a great splash.

The shock of the cold water took my breath away. I bobbed my head up, gasping, giving Hig a giant encouraging grin as I swam toward shore.

I don't think I've ever seen water so deep and clear. Thirty feet below the rippled surface, rocky ledges were strewn with gravel and sunken twigs. Below them, cliffs dropped farther into deep cold blue, disappearing into infinity, with no hint of the bottom. We named it "Floating Vertigo Lake."

From the peak above the lake, we could see granite shelves on the ridge below us, a string of glittering lakes in the valley beyond, the grey and green ridges of our island stretching off into the haze, a far-off clear cut, snowcapped peaks tinted blue with distance, and a much closer swarm of bugs.

The tiny crystal pools pockmarking the poorly drained soil around us provided perfect breeding grounds for the insects. Their tiny bodies swirled in front of the camera lens, and I clicked the shutter twice for each scenic photo, hoping I could edit out the brown blurs later. Despite the bugs—and the cliché nature of the sentiment—it was impossible to feel anything but wonder at the scene.

"Why don't people hike up here?" I asked, kneeling down to frame a burst of lupines and a snowcapped peak.

"Well, if you only have nautical charts, these are the great uncharted wilds…," Hig mused. "Here, there be dragons."

"Loggers don't want it, yachters don't want it, miners don't want it…," I ticked them off, looking around at our lonely alpine wonderland. Some parts of Princess Royal were protected. Others were not. Where we stood was nearly right on the line. But in the granite and tundra, it didn't matter.

"It's just wilderness," Hig finished.

I smiled. "Just for us."

4. ANCIENT WAYS

Erin: "What's wrong with dynamite?"
Hig: "Leaves a paper trail."

FIVE DAYS EARLIER, just before our visit to Princess Royal Island, we had resupplied at the small native village of Klemtu, on Swindle Island, home to the Kitasoo/Xai'xais tribe.

We were sitting in the tiny cafe beside the grocery store, attempting to choke down a huge pile of mediocre french fries. Turning to our neighbor at the table, Hig tried to start a conversation about fish farms. The man's grizzled brown face turned a deep rusty red at the mention of the topic.

"They're always blaming the fish farms," he grumbled darkly, cutting off the conversation before it had a chance to begin.

Up through the Broughton Archipelago, we had seen fenced-in pens of Atlantic salmon tucked into nearly every inlet. Just one salmon farm releases enough waste into the water to equal the untreated sewage of a city of 20,000 to 65,000. Salmon are carnivores. For every pound of farm-raised salmon, three pounds of wild fish must be caught and used to feed them. Farmed fish are fed pink and orange dyes so their naturally pale flesh will mimic the rosy color wild salmon get from the krill in their diet. And farmed salmon have toxic PCB levels over ten times greater than their wild cousins, as well as increased levels of other carcinogens such as dioxin and flame retardants.

Non-native Atlantic salmon escape from the pens, potentially contaminating or competing with the wild Pacific stocks. In the wild

Blueberry bushes grow from drowned trees in a dammed lake at Surf Inlet.

salmon's natural lifecycle, adults are far out in the ocean when the young fish first migrate to the sea. This separation protects the youngsters from diseases they are too small to handle. But when wild salmon smolts migrate past fish farms, they can pick up lethal doses of sea lice from the bigger fish, killing up to 95 percent of the youngsters. In the fish farm riddled Broughton Archipelago, sea lice have decimated as many as 80 percent of the pink salmon runs in the past few decades.

It had been weeks since we'd seen our last salmon farm. We were in northern coastal British Columbia now, where the farms were largely absent. But Klemtu has a salmon farm—bringing $1.5 million dollars to this small community each year. And most of the locals are more than fed up with defending their choice.

We chatted with Doug Neasloss at the Klemtu town dock, where he was standing on the back of his moored boat, casting for the salmon jumping in the bay. A local native guy about our age, Doug worked as the bear-viewing guide in the village, guiding photographers from all over the world along the twisting bear trails near the beaches and salmon streams.

The conversation started with bear stories. We had a few of our own, but were soon enthralled by his tales of being caught in a tense triangle between an irresponsible client and two bears, of a bear going fishing by running in circles and belly flopping into the stream, of Doug being left to babysit cubs by a mother Kermode bear....

Doug had been heavily involved in land- and marine-use planning for his tribe. According to him, Klemtu's fish farm might well be the most environmentally friendly fish farm in Canada. He said they'd solved the escapement problem with special nets from China. They reduced waste and disease by walling off the farms with tarps, placing them in fast tidal currents, and using less feed. They put the farms farther from where the wild smolts migrate, and send three divers per month down to check for damage. The community has the ability to shut down the farm if there's any environmental damage, but Doug doubts it would ever happen—there's too much money involved.

Nothing's perfect. Even the best possible fish farm is still using wild fish stocks as feed, and still releasing waste into the ocean. And when the harvested farm fish leave Klemtu, they go to the same processing plant and appear on grocery store shelves in the same packaging as all the other farmed salmon—the best possible fish farm indistinguishable from the worst.

. . .

Walking down Klemtu's main street, we ran into the same middle-aged man who hadn't wanted to talk about fish farms. This time he was sporting a broad grin. He held a bulging shopping bag in each hand, the bright red and purple spines of sea urchins poking through the thin white plastic.

Hig cornered him on the gravel street, brimming with questions. "How do you prepare them?"

"You eat them raw," he replied simply.

"The whole thing?"

"The orange parts. The eggs. Well, some people eat the seaweed inside, but I don't. Some people say you have to get used to them, but I've liked them since I was a little boy."

He continued down the street, off to prepare a wild food dinner. Apparently he was one of the few. Later, as we chatted further with Doug, he lamented the loss of the village's native food traditions.

"When I was a kid, people still ate a lot more traditional foods. They usually had a deer or a seal hanging that they'd hunted. Every day in the summer, people would go out. Get seaweed. Get clams. Harvest something. All in a big group."

He gestured around at the harbor, mostly empty but for a few tourist yachts. "Now no one has boats. They sold them when the cannery closed. A few people still go out and set nets, but the logistics are difficult. I can count on one hand the number of people who still eat native foods."

"You know, Princess Royal Island used to have a village at the mouth of every stream. This whole area did. Now we're the only ones left."

In a way, this is the story of many of the places we traveled through. Coastlines once speckled with communities are now largely forsaken, depopulated first by disease, and now suffering from chronic emigration.

The forces of culture and economics draw people away from these remote rural areas, concentrating them into larger towns and cities connected to the road net.

. . .

At Surf Inlet, we were beyond the protected swath of Princess Royal Island, in an area of the island that had long been open to industry.

"How do we know they didn't just go off for the day?" Hig wondered, peering through the dusty window of an empty trailer.

"There's mold on the table."

I strode into the dark musty space, taking only a moment to note the calendar on the table (June 2005—only two years old!) before I started wrenching open every cupboard door I could find, searching for anything still edible. I grabbed pasta, jerky, and Wheat Thins, sniffing the boxes, looking for signs of water damage, quickly accumulating a pile of much-wanted calories in my arms. Hig mumbled something about the failing light, trying to hurry us back to our camp.

"Don't you think we should raid food?" I asked, surprised. We'd been lamenting our short rations for days already.

"Yes, but...places like this creep me out."

"What's creepy about an abandoned logging camp?"

"Old sketchy trailers...," Hig mumbled.

"Old sketchy trailers that have food!"

"Yeah."

We built a bonfire of left-behind firewood, cooking left-behind pasta at our camp near a couple of left-behind trucks. The story we'd heard was that Surf Inlet was once the site of a mining town of a couple thousand people, abandoned in World War II. But the abandoned trailers, piles of trash, and leaking barrels of who-knows-what were evidence of a more recent occupation.

Just up the bay, the crumbling concrete hulk of an old mining building perched on pillars above the intertidal zone. Alder and hemlock saplings grew through the gaps where its windows had been, seeking light between the remains of rusted iron bars. A pipe big enough for a bear to crawl through dangled from the edge of the building, perhaps an old tunnel for mining slurry. I stood on tiptoe on the seaweed-covered rocks, reached over my head for a rusted piece of rebar, and pulled myself onto a rotten piling, and then onto a weighty concrete beam. I walked along the over-wide balance beam, stepping over pieces of broken glass, ducking through one of the window gaps. Roof beams littered the floor. Nails poked out of painted scraps of wood. The mining operation at Surf Inlet had been abandoned for over sixty years. The town had melted away in the quick rot of wood in a rainforest. Only the concrete and metal stood as a reminder. And the dam.

A waterfall roared over the top of a concrete spillway, tumbling in a white rush into the inlet below. Behind the dam, what had once been a chain of three large lakes was now one giant one. Hawks nested on the tops of drowned snags polished white with time, while blueberry bushes and hemlock saplings grew from crevices in the old trunks, precariously suspended over the dark green water.

We paddled through the drowned forest, squeezing into packraft-sized gaps between logs, photographing the dead trees against the logging on the hillside. Clear-cut patches decorated the slopes, set beneath monstrous granite cliffs, behind a shifting curtain of picturesque clouds. The lakes were named "Cougar," "Bear," and "Deer," but we saw no wildlife beyond the hawks. Fresh-looking flagging tape hung near fresh-looking clear cuts, with "Special Management Zone" printed in black block letters against the orange.

Once, this must have been an amazing area for wildlife. The string of lakes would have been perfect for sockeye salmon to spawn, connected by short riffles perfect for bears to catch them. Perfect for people to catch them as well. No one we talked to was old enough to remember the lakes person-ally, but when we reached Hartley Bay, the next village up the coast, people told us about the huge salmon runs that used to return to the now empty spawning grounds. Before the logging camp, before the mining town, Surf Inlet surely was home to one of those long-lost villages that once dotted the shores of Princess Royal. I tried to picture native inhabitants of centuries past, strips of thick red salmon flesh hanging from their drying racks. But no fish could get past that dam.

The dam felt like a slap in the face. It seemed as though someone was preventing the return of the salmon for no reason at all.

"I wonder what's the most low tech way you could blow up this dam," Hig mused as we paddled.

"What's wrong with dynamite?"

"Leaves a paper trail."

I laughed. "What, you're thinking of doing it ourselves? I don't think you'd need to be sneaky. You could officially blow up this dam. I mean, who's getting anything out of it now?"

We couldn't see a reason. It wasn't generating power. And the mining operation that had created the dam had long since disappeared.

Hig busied himself during the long crossing by brainstorming new and creative ways to destroy the dam. His possible solutions included growing trees on it, smashing logs into it, building plywood walls to raise the water and collapse it, starting giant fires below the dam, shattering the concrete with thermite.... His favorite involved anchoring a boom chain so that it sat in the fast-moving water of the spillway. The water would rattle the heavy chain, causing it to chew slowly through the concrete until the dam failed. The flood that followed would leave no evidence that the failure had been anything other than natural.

Later, talking to a man from Hartley Bay, we found that there was a reason for the dam. The logging company working the shores of those lakes found it easier to float the logs out with the dam still intact. They weren't logging now, but just in case they logged again, they wanted the dam left there. When there was nothing left to log, then they might decommission it. There were vague plans for a fish ladder, but as we'd seen in Salmon Inlet, no guarantee and no hurry to make it happen. I wondered why there wasn't any hurry. Between dams, salmon farms, overfishing, and streamside logging, British Columbia's wild salmon had already declined to just a third of their historic levels.

I tried to imagine the days when the dams were created. Back then, the supply of salmon must have seemed infinite. Streams and rivers could be haphazardly blocked off, without a passing thought to the future of the fish.

But in addition to the dam, the loggers had left behind some much-appreciated food. I munched on a two-year-old Wheat Thin as we headed off for our next point of resupply at Hartley Bay village.

Every day, each of us consumed two pounds of food. Added to our twenty pounds of gear, each day's rations made our backpacks more and more unmanageable. Almost as much as the terrain, the logistical challenges of planning the journey revolved around food.

We had worked hard to get the weight of our daily ration down to two pounds. Fat packs a greater caloric punch than starch or protein—over twice the calories for the weight. So we ate as much fat as our bodies could handle—melting a stick of butter into every cooked meal, filling up on snacks of cheese, chocolate, cookies, and potato chips.

Nearly half our pre-trip research centered on resupply points. Where could we get more food? We divided our entire route into "legs" between those outposts—thinking of distance not in miles, but in food-days. The volume of our packs and the strength of our backs limited us to a maximum load of about two weeks' food. At an average speed of around thirteen miles a day, two weeks would take us almost two hundred miles. But terrain was rarely average—we might make only five miles in a day of tough bush-whacking, or over thirty on a fast-flowing river.

We didn't often carry a full two weeks of food—only just enough to get us to the next grocery store. So each time the terrain became more difficult, making one of our "legs" take longer than expected, we shrunk our rations. Often desperately hungry upon our return to civilization, we had to eat what we could get.

· · ·

We clomped onto the back porch of a small house in Hartley Bay, a tiny First Nations community and home of the Gitga'at tribe, about seventy-five miles southeast of Prince Rupert. I shuffled my feet nervously as Hig knocked on the door. "Is this really the store?"

It was. A woman opened the door, and we stepped inside to a heart-sinking view. Directly in front of me was a half-empty shelf of snack-size potato chip bags. Next to that, a fridge full of pop. And by the desk, a small

array of Oh Henry! candy bars. My mind started racing as I pulled bags
of chips off the shelf, examining the nutritional information on the back
and lining them up in 1000-calorie rows. At a couple dollars per bag, these
would quickly break our eleven dollar per-person daily food budget. But
that might be OK for a single resupply. And it might even be OK to live
on nothing but candy and chips for a while. But it was a moot point. We
needed seven days worth of food to take us to Prince Rupert. In the whole
store, I doubted if there was even three.

People in Hartley Bay had to eat something other than chips, pop, and
candy. We discovered that they got these other foodstuffs from a grocery
store in Prince Rupert, delivered via North Pacific Seaplanes.

Mist and clouds swirled in the mountains behind town the next
morning. The trash collector passed by, pulling a trailer behind his
four-wheeler on the boardwalk, rapidly filling it with plastic bags. I sat
cross-legged on a bench, poring over maps of the next leg's journey, waiting for the 9 AM plane.

Eventually we migrated over to the cafe—just a small house with a
couple of tables set out on the porch. Drinking coffee, I watched the sky,
listening to the cafe owner's cheery lambasting of the seaplane company.

"Oh, sometimes I have to wait three or four days for my stuff.
Sometimes they drop it off somewhere else. They're not very bright over at
North Pacific Seaplanes. They don't like me anymore."

Hig raced off at the first sound of a plane engine, only to find that
an hour earlier, the plane had left Prince Rupert without our box of food.
Apparently, "Erin" had been on the box, and "McKittrick" on the credit
card receipt. Since they didn't know of an Erin in Hartley Bay, and couldn't
figure out if the shipping had been paid, they left the box behind.

In the end, the best thing we could do was scrounge through the cafe
owner's cupboards, as he generously offered to sell us whatever he had that
was dry and nonperishable. We paddled off toward the Quaal River valley
with backpacks full of peach-flavored drink mix and American cheese.

. . .

The world was black. My headlamp made pools of pale white light on our piles of strewn gear. I stuffed it all into my pack, and blew a last few breaths of air into my packraft.

The world was grey. A few nearby rocks poked out of the water. Beyond them, the water was a smooth colorless sheet, transitioning seamlessly from grey inlet to a foggy grey sky, leaving the rest of the landscape shrouded. We launched, paddling softly into the mystery.

The world was pink. The dark silhouettes of mountains peered out from the fog, standing against the dawning day. Distant peaks were tinged pink where they touched the sun, and the blanket of fog was slowly separating into wisps of nothing. The tide carried us up into the mouth of the Quaal River, still deeply shadowed in the bottom of the valley.

The world was golden. We stood on a small island in the middle of the river, dewy grass and spiderwebs sparkling in the first beams of the sun. I took off my hood in the sudden warmth. We slowly circled the island, looking for signs of its unusual history.

This island wasn't natural. The grass leaving our legs wet with dew, the moss-covered spruce trees—everything grew on an artificial platform. Fifteen miles up Douglas Channel from Hartley Bay, this was an older village site of the Gitga'at tribe. Long ago, the native people who lived here had dragged rot-resistant yellow cedar logs down from the mountains, arranged them on the bottom of the river and built up land where none had been. On this island, they dug pits and constructed a dozen houses. When other tribes raided their village on shore, the women and children sheltered here, on their refuge island.

Before airplanes and powerboats, a major trading route led up the Quaal River valley, connecting over a low pass to the Ecstall River valley on the other side. Nobody had walked that route in decades. But we planned to follow it—walking up the Quaal and floating down the Ecstall. For packrafters, it was still the perfect way.

Following the Quaal River upstream, our noses were assailed by the many flavors of rotting salmon. Salmon freshly dead on the gravel banks, piles of decayed salmon goo crawling with maggots, half-eaten salmon heads, piles of bear scat built entirely from rotting salmon, and spawned-out salmon decaying as they swam, all mixed with the rich odor of stink-currant bushes lining the river.

Wading across a shallow channel, we set off a frenzy of terrified splashing, the humped backs of pink salmon waving above the water, knifing their way upstream. The less careful fish ricocheted off our calves. A flock of seagulls took off upstream. I glanced in their direction to see what scared them and met the eyes of a black bear. She looked at me for a second, and then ran, black rump crashing into the bushes. We saw only one bear. But I wouldn't be surprised if at least ten had seen, heard, or smelled us.

The Quaal River valley is an amazingly diverse ecosystem, different from any other forest we'd encountered. Monstrous spruce trees towered over thickets of stink-currant and salmonberry bushes, growing in the oddly straight rows left by long-gone nurse logs. At least eight feet in diameter, these were some of the largest trees we'd seen on this journey. Circular patches worn into the dirt at their roots were the campsites of bears. For the first time in British Columbia, we saw meadows of cloudberries, which we knew mainly from northern tundra realms. Two other new berry species appeared alongside them. In the gullies, skunk cabbage grew so thick and luxuriously large that one leaf could have made a person's umbrella. Yew trees, which are rare everywhere else I've been, speckled the forest. We balanced precariously on the tops of beaver dams, weaving through the ponded and marshy world. With such a wealth of life, it was obvious why this valley had been chosen as a home by the long-ago natives.

At the head of the valley, we followed a steep and furrowed trail, angling up the slope toward the pass. We walked in the well-worn footprints of bears. But this wasn't an animal trail. Animal trails are straightforward. Rather than seeking the least brushy, least precarious, or least steep route, bears usually follow the most obvious and direct one—right along the banks of a river, right on the edge of a cliff, or right up the axis of a pass. This trail was obviously smarter. Instead of charging straight up to the pass, it snuck along the top of a shelf, taking a clever and more efficient approach. This trail didn't reflect the methodical mind of ursine trailblazers—it was human.

Of course, no trail is ever just a human trail. Bears and moose stomp down the routes used by humans, and humans improve the routes walked by animals—coexisting in this landscape for thousands of years.

I wondered how many centuries this particular trail stretched into the past. Thrilled by the sense of discovery, we continued hiking past dark, eager to discover where the ancient path would lead. Walking in the steps of those who had created this route and knew it well, I imagined them carrying oolichan grease on their backs for trade, speaking languages now largely forgotten.

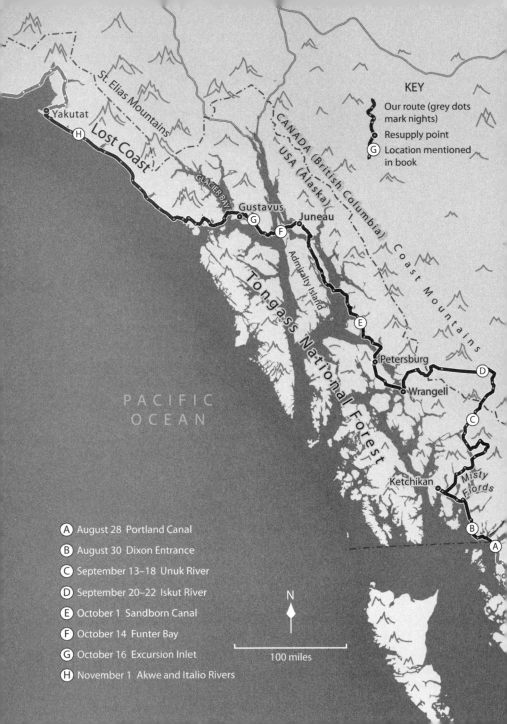

KEY

Our route (grey dots mark nights)

Resupply point

G Location mentioned in book

St. Elias Mountains

Yakutat

H Lost Coast

GLACIER BAY

Gustavus

G

Juneau

F

CANADA (British Columbia)
USA (Alaska)

Coast Mountains

Admiralty Island

Tongass National Forest

E

Petersburg

Wrangell

D

C

PACIFIC
OCEAN

Ketchikan

Misty Fiords

B

A

A August 28 Portland Canal

B August 30 Dixon Entrance

C September 13–18 Unuk River

D September 20–22 Iskut River

E October 1 Sandborn Canal

F October 14 Funter Bay

G October 16 Excursion Inlet

H November 1 Akwe and Italio Rivers

N

100 miles

FALL

[AUGUST 28–NOVEMBER 7]

837 MILES

5. ROUGH WATER, STEEP MOUNTAINS

Hig: "We can see a little way into that tight spot,
and it doesn't look too bad...."

NAMES FLOWED THROUGH my brain. Names of mountains and rivers, of islands and bays. We'd pored over them on digital maps, not even knowing how the majority of them were pronounced. Most left our brains as soon as they arrived. A few stuck: Portland Canal, Yakutat Bay, Icy Bay, Copper River, Knik Arm, False Pass.

Each of these was a packraft crossing—but not one that straddled protected inland waters, like our seven-mile paddle to Vancouver Island. These crossings were exposed to the open seas—to the full force of whatever the weather could bring. And each one was a sticking point. In other crossings, we had a choice: paddle or walk. Not here. If we couldn't paddle, the way around was either very long or nonexistent.

Portland Canal was the first of these crossings, a four-mile-wide finger of water extending ninety miles inland just south of the border between British Columbia and Alaska. Here, the Inside Passage has an outer door. No islands stand between these shores and the storms and swells of the open ocean. The gap invites the wind, which rushes forward to meet the tidal currents that race along the channel. And at the speed of a packraft, the four-mile crossing promised to be at least a two-hour paddle—plenty of time for conditions to change.

Packrafting in front of a waterfall on Lake Creek in Alaska's Misty Fiords

...

We bobbed up and down in the small swells, staring across the expanse. A fisherman had given us the weather forecast—a forty-knot gale blowing up from the southeast. The wind was supposed to have arrived two hours ago.

It was calm. Barely breezy. But there was no pause in our paddle strokes as we hurried across Portland Canal, watching the sky. If the gale came, the wind would be blowing right behind us. A tailwind could help us on our way. But a tailwind could also build the small swells into dangerous waves. I knew we could reenter the rafts if we were knocked out. And I knew the packrafts had a remarkable ability to ride over waves. I just wasn't sure what their limits were.

I was confident that our plan was a safe one. Nevertheless, when we hit the three-quarters mark without a hint of wind, I breathed a sigh of relief. As the last bit of adrenaline faded, the exhaustion and discomfort I'd pushed to the back of my mind began to draw more and more of my attention.

Dark was falling on the islands around us. Our proposed landing point quickly receded to our right, as the outgoing tide pulled us farther and farther toward the open sea. I tried to tell myself that it was a good thing. The tide was pulling us west and we needed to go west anyway. Anywhere this current took us would cut off distance from our paddle tomorrow, as long as it didn't pull us all the way out into the open ocean. That was a long distance off, and I wasn't worried. But I was tired. A curtain of rain descended, reducing our visibility even further. All we could see of the world were the smudgy grey outlines of nearby islands, silhouetted against the slightly lighter sky.

Then the current switched—and instead of making westward progress, we were being dragged back up the channel. Our two-mile-an-hour paddling seemed feeble compared to the forces pushing us around.

It was 10:30 PM, three hours since the start of our crossing and an hour past darkness, when I finally heard the sound of small waves crashing on rocks. It was the sound of home. Unfortunately, I could see neither waves, nor rocks, nor shore. It was pitch dark and still raining. In the faint beam of my headlamp, I could barely discern a narrow passageway: a channel through seaweed and barnacle-covered rocks to a cobble beach behind the reef. Four glowing orbs beamed back at me from the top of a rock—the eyes of a pair of low-tide beachcombers. We rode our packrafts into shore, suddenly thrown off balance by the solid rocks beneath us and the sudden cessation of the boats' gentle swaying. I staggered from my raft, stiff-legged and awkward, stumbling toward the promised shelter of a forest camp.

Our first major crossing was behind us.

· · ·

Here at the end of August, we passed through two invisible boundaries. We had reached the end of the summer. The days were getting shorter. The breezes were getting chillier. Rain showers came more frequently, and the sun's brief appearances became rare enough that I started noting them in my journal. We had begun the slow, inexorable descent into winter cold and winter dark, and it would be a long time before we came out the other side.

The other boundary was political. In a forest-lined channel that looked just like every other inlet, a thick dashed line on our map ran invisibly over the dark blue water.

I looked up from the map, turning to Hig. "Ready to go to Alaska? Or would you like to stay in Canada a bit longer?"

"I'm getting homesick. Let's go."

Somewhere in between those dark green shores, I took the paddle stroke that finished the first quarter of our journey: one thousand miles traveled, and three thousand more to go.

· · ·

It was two days beyond Portland Canal before we saw the promised gale. And while we'd crossed our fingers and prayed for its delay in the Portland Canal crossing, we welcomed it here on the waters of Revillagigedo Channel.

We met the storm while paddling along a rocky coast facing the open expanse of Dixon Entrance. Each time we went around a point, the waves steepened. We paddled out, threading our way around the barely submerged rocks and the foaming breaks that crashed over them. In the biggest sets, the waves must have been nearly six feet high, sending the rafts bouncing between tall pinnacles and deep, grey-blue holes. Squalls of rain passed over us, alternating with brief sunspots. I paddled with my head craned over my left shoulder, watching the waves roll in behind me.

In a packraft, the paddler's eyes sit two-and-a-half feet above the water. Any nearby wave of that same height rises into the sky, cutting off the smooth line of the horizon. Behind a bigger wave, nearly the whole world disappears.

Spotting the curling white line of a large breaking wave, I watched it advance behind me, holding my course until the last possible second. As the crest began to lift my raft, I gave a quick flick of my paddle to align myself with its motion, riding over the break in the most stable way possible. The tail wind sent me flying. It was nerve-racking and exhilarating. But it was safe.

Paddling around wave-battered rocks, we peered through narrow gaps and passageways, occasionally catching a glimpse of a tucked-in sandy beach. Each pocket of sand was an escape valve. The waves bounced and reflected through the maze of boulders, losing energy with every turn. The roiling breaks couldn't survive the journey to these pocket beaches. They were islands of calm in a blustery world.

We waved cheerfully at a passing fishing boat, then watched with wry amusement as it ducked into a protected bay and dropped anchor as we sailed onward in our tiny yellow rafts. No one had ever brought a packraft through these waters, though kayakers often ply them. It had been generations since people traveled much of this country on foot. It was left to us to determine, situation by situation and step by step, what could be safely done. With land so near, and the wind at our backs, it was the perfect place to stretch our boundaries—to test the limits of packrafts in ocean storms. To prepare for the fall to come.

. . .

A few days later, we arrived in Ketchikan, where we stayed with a pair of newly met friends. The local newspaper caught up to us while I was making a pasta salad in our hosts' kitchen. The reporter flipped open his notepad and began interviewing us as we worked on dinner.

"You have a writing background. I bet you have a good, quick way of encapsulating the idea of this trip." He waited expectantly, pen poised over the blank page.

"Ummm…" Hig and I looked at each other.

I was far from being comfortable as a public figure. How could we encapsulate such a broad and far-reaching idea? How could we explain everything we'd seen, much less all we hoped to learn and share, in a couple of words?

Every time I talked to the media, I felt an inherent contradiction. We wanted to talk to them because we thought what we were doing was wonderful, and hopefully meaningful. They wanted to talk to us because they thought what we were doing was nuts. Standing in Southeast Alaska in September, proclaiming an intent to walk to the Aleutians…it sounded more than a little bit crazy.

I knew I wasn't a thrill seeker. I knew that the situations we faced every day were for us—familiar with the wilderness—no more dangerous than driving a car was for the people we talked to. This trip wasn't about how crazy we were. It wasn't even supposed to be about us. We bumbled our way along, giving an explanation that was neither good nor quick. I felt embarrassed, sure that real public figures would have figured out better sound bites.

• • •

With Ketchikan behind us, we paddled north on Carroll Inlet, heading for a crossing of Revillagigedo Island. Once on land, we followed a well-maintained forest service road up Marble Creek, but beyond the end of the white gravel ribbon, nothing could help us. Logging debris was everywhere. Discarded branches and logs lay underfoot, dried hard and spiked with the sharp ends of smaller branches. A profusion of bushes grew over the top; bright red huckleberries and deep-blue blueberries hanging from heavy branches, obscuring the tricky footing beneath. A shower of rain fell from each bush as my legs brushed against it. Even the bears' heavy feet couldn't make a dent in the brush. With no trail to follow, we barreled through the tangled bushes, trying to force them out of our way. I wished I were as strong and streamlined as a bear.

We were bushwhacking our way across a tiny section of the Tongass National Forest. The Tongass encompasses 80 percent of Southeast

Alaska—a panhandle of coastal mountains, inlets, and islands that stretches north from the border with British Columbia. Here, storms and clouds from the Pacific crash into towering mountains. Ice fields form among massive peaks, sending glacial fingers down toward the sea. Below the mountains, copious rains and year-round mists soak the land. In the rains grow towering evergreens—enormous cedar, spruce, and hemlock—draped in blankets of dripping moss. The Tongass is the northern extension of the Great Bear Rainforest, separated only by a political boundary.

But the iconic, towering trees of a temperate rainforest are rare in the Tongass. Though this particular national forest spans seventeen million acres, much of it isn't forest. Two thirds of the area is covered in ice, rock, tundra, brush, bogs, or meadows. Much of the rest sports only spindly trees.

In the Tongass, even trees can drown. Thin layers of soil drape impermeable granite rock, pooling the incessant rain. Spruce and hemlock drown, leaving muskeg meadows of sphagnum moss, scrubby yellow cedars, and twisted pines—a beautiful landscape, but not a forest. Sometimes a single line of trees will stand alone in a marsh, the legacy of an ancient nurse log that once supported young saplings above the wet soil. Large trees cling to patches of porous rock, growing on piles of talus, on stripes of marble, or in the base of the region's larger valleys. If the old-growth forest was an ancient city, then these trees were its ramparts, its monuments and temples.

In the Tongass today, much of what remains unlogged are the more tree-poor districts. The logging companies cut the most productive areas first, because their ecological richness produced the biggest stands of trees. Typically, those areas were in the valleys, which were not only the best habitats for trees, but also the richest and most valuable habitats for all life in the forest.

It's easy for someone who cares about forests to get caught up in numbers, such as how many acres of pristine wilderness have been saved from chainsaws. On paper, the Tongass National Forest includes millions of acres of untouched wilderness. But does this translate into forest? "Pristine" doesn't always mean ecologically important. Most of the untouched areas of the Tongass consist of steep granite cliffs, impressive glaciers, and alpine meadows.

All are pristine. But if such areas were opened to logging right now? No one would be clamoring for the twisted, five-foot-tall trees surviving on the windy ridge tops. Meanwhile, some of the most important places to save—the once-forested homes of bear and deer and spawning salmon—those are no longer pristine.

But such areas will eventually rejuvenate. Trees will regrow. The monuments will return. If we really want healthy forests and habitat for future generations, we need to protect those places that were logged long ago. As difficult as it is to get excited about the "leftovers," maybe that's what we most need to protect.

. . .

But as we bushwhacked through the remaining forests, it wasn't the trees that caught my attention.

Devil's club is a beautiful plant. Platter-sized leaves perch improbably on crooked woody stems, forming a bright green canopy above the forest floor. In fall, each plant gains a stalk of bright-red berries, food for bears and other wild creatures. It's a rainforest native. It's a ginseng relative, thought to have medicinal properties. People grow it as an ornamental in their gardens. And I absolutely detest it.

Thick and vicious on every woody stem, and hidden on the underside of every leaf, tiny spines coat every surface of the beastly beast. The insidious spines worm their way through socks, through fleece, through heavy-duty raincoats, through everything short of armor. Once they've breached these outer defenses, they lodge themselves in human skin, releasing their special toxin. Within a few days, each tiny prick becomes a sore and festering lump, closed tightly over a hair-thin spine. The spines are nearly impossible to dig out until they fester.

Walking through the devil's club-ridden rainforest, I plotted their demise, imagining a genetically engineered pestilence that would wipe them from the earth. Thicker-skinned than me, Hig laughed at the intensity of my hatred, kindly hacking a few of the evil plants out of the way with his ice ax. It wasn't fair. He'd grown up crawling through devil's club in Southcentral Alaska. He was immune. I reminded him that he would be at *least* as unreasonable if we were thrashing through hordes of mosquitoes rather than thickets of devil's club.

We were traversing our way along a steep valley wall that seemed to get steeper and brushier with every step. My foot missed the ground, landing instead on a bundle of salmonberry canes, which scooted out from under me. I shot out my arms as I fell, landing with one hand squarely on the stem of a devil's club.

On my knees in the mud, I fruitlessly tried to pick spines from my palm. Devil's club: twenty. Erin: zero.

• • •

In the overgrown and convoluted Misty Fiords National Monument—a world of cliffs and rainforest—no way was straightforward. Glacially carved granite mountains plunged into fjords in a cascade of waterfalls. Turquoise glacial rivers braided and wove across remote valley floors. Steep cliffs— impossible to climb—walled off potential passes. And where it was possible to walk, a thick profusion of brush often tangled the route. It was beautifully impenetrable. And we weren't making it any easier on ourselves.

Between Ketchikan and Wrangell, our path was one giant detour. The simplest way would have taken us just a little bit west of north, through inland waterways and over one low pass—about a hundred miles. Instead, we chose to go 275 miles: northeast through Misty Fiords and then farther east and farther inland, crossing back into Canada on the Unuk River, into a remote volcanic area of mountains known to miners as the Golden Triangle. From there we would float—following the Iskut River until it joined the Stikine, spitting us back into the sea just a few miles from Wrangell.

I puzzled over detail maps of the passes we thought we'd cross, and large-area maps of places we never thought we'd be, analyzing intricate unknowns and potential stopping points, ever aware of our limited food supplies. And along the way, we made small detour after small detour, each one making our path a little longer—each one irresistible.

• • •

We relaxed under a warm golden sun on a three-thousand-foot peak, watching the tide go out on the Unuk River far below us. According to the calculations we had made less than twenty-four hours ago, we should have been a good way up that river already. But we'd ignored our own advice.

Meadowy shelves had led us up and down through cracks in the mounded granite, across squelching golden moss and sprays of plants starting to turn orange with the fall. We had cruised toward the peak, topless, sweating under a blazing September sun, enjoying the feeling of being strong and working hard. I rubbed my head with handfuls of last year's snow.

"Since we're a day behind anyway," Hig began, "maybe we should just camp here. I'd love to see the sunset from this peak."

We brought out the maps again, convincing ourselves that even with this alpine detour it would take us only another week to get to Wrangell. We brought out our food bags, convincing ourselves that we would have something to eat for that week.

On a long journey, efficiency plays tug-of-war with inspiration. There's a magic in losing sight of the grander goal, in putting off the eventual triumphant completion of the journey to go somewhere just because it looks amazing.

So we pulled each other farther and farther from practicality—an interaction at the heart of all our adventures. I had pushed for the whole 4,000-mile journey. I had pushed for the long detour into Misty Fiords and the Golden Triangle. Along the way, Hig had pushed for nearly every small adventure—over the peak we stood on, and down each path that was potentially more difficult but potentially more amazing. People we met along the way often asked how Hig had convinced me to join him on this trip. They rarely wondered the reverse. They wanted to slot us into neat categories of "leader" and "follower." But it was silly. Without our interaction, I knew that neither of us would be here.

We kept winding and weaving. From the Unuk River, we detoured to the dramatic waterfall at the head of Lake Creek, where towering cascades thundered into a pool, plunging nearly a hundred feet from the sky. We detoured to the Blue River's legendary "boot-eating" lava. It was as sharp and fresh as was promised—a plain of fractured lava covered in a several-inch

layer of springy moss. And we continued in the wrong direction, detouring
northeast into the Golden Triangle.

. . .

Lava flows ooze out across the Iskut and Unuk river valleys, choking the
rivers into deep canyons of columnar rock. Above the gorges, collapsed lava
tubes pockmark the mossy forest floor, sending chill air flowing out of deep
cracks. The forests are young; a natural second growth of skinny trees, with
only mushrooms and moss growing in the dark understory.

In the first lava gorge, the Unuk's gravel bars disappeared. We walked
in the forest, on a miner's roadbed long since overgrown with a lush carpet
of devil's club. Occasional pieces of rusted and moss-covered machinery, a
broken down cable crossing on a river, and an unusually straight track were
all that marked this dirt path as anything more than another animal trail.

Beneath this upheaval of rocks lies a glitter of gold, driving modern
prospecting as it drove the old-time fortune seekers. People have been looking for gold in these hills since the arrival of the white man over a hundred
years ago. Only the scale has changed.

. . .

Packrafts in hand, we stood at the edge of the opaque yellow water of
Sulphurets Creek, eyeing the mining exploration camp on the other side.
A helicopter sat near a small collection of buildings. We hadn't spotted any
people, but we could hear the steady hum of a generator. Obviously, someone was home.

"I think we should stop in and chat," Hig suggested.

"Sure…," I replied hesitantly. "Only maybe we should play down our
greenness a little. That might increase the chance of them giving us food."

As Hig inflated his packraft to cross the creek, I stuck my hand
into the greasy ziploc bag at the top of my pack, pulling out a handful of
"Buttery Goodness." Utterly sick of store-bought cookies, we had become
more inventive in our resupplies. Our new favorite creation was a raw
mishmash of butter, oats, sugar, and cinnamon, which tasted exactly like
oatmeal cookie dough. We dubbed it "Buttery Goodness." We'd replaced
our meals of soup packets with a heavenly macaroni and cheese—full of

real cheese and butter, with wild mushrooms, garlic, and a touch of curry powder. But nothing could change the basic math. Food was heavy, and as the difficult terrain lengthened all our detours, we found we weren't carrying nearly enough.

As we approached the mining camp on the far side of the creek, a small group of men came out to greet us. We'd barely finished explaining what we were up to when Steve, the camp manager, proceeded to offer us everything we could possibly want. Our environmental leanings were entirely irrelevant. We had a place to stay for the night. We had showers. We had food!

"We're pretty much all hikers and mountaineers out here anyway," Steve explained, "so we understand."

"Wow. Thanks."

Clean, refreshed, and happily steaming, I padded out of the shower room. Steve was there, waiting to ambush us with an official-looking piece of paper.

"Yeah, well, I'm just covering my ass," he explained, handing us the nondisclosure agreement.

Hig and I bent over the paper, reading our fate. Apparently, the price for the shower and hospitality was agreeing never to say anything about this mining company for the rest of our lives. Nothing about its business practices or environmental practices. Not even its name! We were forbidden from even mentioning that the unmentionable mining company had a camp full of very nice employees who had put us up for the night. It made me uncomfortable. I didn't know anything about the company. What if they did something terrible later on? Or great? But for now, they required only that we never mention their name. We decided that our silence was a small price to pay for access to that dining hall....

Several days beyond the friendly and unmentionable mining exploration camp, we stood at a tailings pond of the Eskay Creek Mine—the only currently active mine in the Golden Triangle. A pump and generator whirred away, drawing cloudy water from an artificial lake and returning it to the outlet. All around was a swath of bare gravel, packed down by machinery.

Square plastic tanks were stacked on the shore, labeled as "Sulfuric Acid" and "Enviro-Safe." Hig took pictures. I nervously looked around for any signs of approaching people. We hadn't seen anything telling us not to come this way, but I was sure it wouldn't be allowed.

Steve had bragged to us about the incredibly small footprint of Eskay Creek Mine: "Even smaller than this camp!" But he must have meant only the mine shaft. We'd been following their four-wheeler trails for miles, between disposal ponds, dams, and incomprehensible bits of machinery, and we'd only just popped out onto the end of their seventy-mile gravel road. We never saw the hole. But with roads, power, waste storage, fuel, workers, and transportation, the footprint of any mine is much larger than the spot they dig the rock from.

Relative to other mine proposals, Eskay Creek Mine is tiny. The Golden Triangle is full of prospects—each potential mine upstream of major salmon rivers that flow from British Columbia into Southeast Alaska.

. . .

From the waters of the Iskut River, fluted and undulating columns of lava rose in cliffs a hundred feet high. We stood in the depths of the gorge, packrafts pulled out on the gravel beside us. Water crashed around a giant boulder in the rapid we'd just portaged, roaring in our ears as we discussed the plan ahead.

"We can see a little way into that tight spot, and it doesn't look too bad...," Hig observed.

"But we can't see around the corner," I protested, pointing to the map. "Look, this is only a third of it. And if there is something bad around the corner, we'll have absolutely no way to get out of the river. There's nowhere to land on those cliffs. I think we should try to climb out of the canyon here."

The debate continued back and forth, but there was no getting around the basic uncertainty: What was around that blind corner? Somewhat reluctantly, we packed up the rafts. The float down the canyon had been beautiful so far, and we were both looking forward to continuing downstream. But just ahead and just out of sight, the river narrowed to the tightest spot we could see on the map. Perfect for a deadly rapid.

Our maps were printed on 8½ x 11 inch sheets of waterproof paper—shrunken versions of the USGS one-inch to one-mile maps and their Canadian equivalents. In Seattle, we'd taken our best guess of where we were headed on each leg and had printed out topographic maps for the first 2,500 miles—from Seattle to Anchorage. Every month or so, we'd pick up a new sheaf of maps—mailed to us by my ever-helpful mom. We carried a compass, but used it only in whiteouts, fog, or places where landmarks were truly impossible to see. A tiny GPS recorded our route as we walked, but only a computer could read the data—our simple GPS lacked a screen. We rarely had local intelligence about the places we traveled. The topographic maps were all we had.

Landmarks oriented us, and we navigated using the shape of the land—trying to calculate obstacles such as cliffs and rapids based on the blank spaces between the 100-foot contour lines on our maps. Sometimes, when detours or difficulties took us places we hadn't expected to be, even the maps were missing. Twice already on this leg, we had walked off the edge of our maps. In this gorge of the Iskut River, we had a map, but it was little help. It warned us about the narrow spot in the river, but at map scale, the cliff beside us was nothing more than a dark smudge where two contour lines sat nearly on top of each other.

We split up to scout an escape, trying one way and then another, edging along moss-covered shelves that inevitably dead-ended at the base of a sheer cliff of lava. Two-and-a-half hours later, Hig and I rejoined each other where we'd dumped our packs, sinking down onto boulder seats for another strategic consultation. We were still stuck at the bottom of the canyon. I was starting to feel we were truly trapped—trapped between a cliff and a blind corner. Hidden behind their screen of trees, the cliffs seemed impossible to climb.

We split up again, determined to give it one last try. I tramped back to the base of the slope. On each previous scouting trip, I'd walked right past the thickest patch of devil's club. This time I bit my tongue and charged right into the spiny monsters, stumbling almost immediately on a hidden shelf.

It was a narrow ledge, formed from the broken-off tops of lava columns, angling slowly up the face of an otherwise sheer cliff. In the middle of the shelf, a single tree grew, leaving just enough space to squeeze between its trunk and the cliff behind. I crossed my fingers, sure of another dead end. But this time, the dead end wasn't a sheer slope. This time, it was just a very steep patch of dirt, where scuff marks and the scratches of claws showed how bears trapped in the canyon had used this exact same escape route.

We returned with our packs. I tried to hold vertigo at bay as Hig pulled out the video camera to film my ascent. If the bears could do it, I could do it.

A minute later, we both stood on the rim of the canyon, walking a smooth moss carpet on the flattest and most open forest floor imaginable.

Half an hour later, we had a view into the gorge. The water around our blind corner was utterly smooth. There was no rapid.

6. RAINBOW SEASON

Shrimp fisherman:
"Where's the rest of your boat!?!"

IN WRANGELL, WE sat in a new friend's cozy kitchen, listening to the staccato drumming of rain on the roof as we waited for the marine weather forecast. For a few more weeks, we still would be in the Inside Passage, where steep terrain, intricate bays, and thick bushwhacks pinned us down to a route that was largely marine. But it was already late September, and with each day, we worried that the window of paddling season was closing. The business-like voice of the forecaster issued from the radio. Wind from the southeast, increasing to twenty-five knots by the afternoon. At least it would be at our backs.

When we weren't in a town, we had no access to a weather forecast. But I wasn't sure the information really helped. We'd been in Wrangell for two days and were already anxious to get out again. At that moment, it looked calm. So we launched, pointing our stubby yellow boats toward Mitkof Island, somewhere behind the mist.

For more than three months, we had dressed in experimental dry suits donated to us by our packraft company, wearing them on all but the hottest days. Waterproof and breathable, the coat and pants sealed together, putting them somewhere between a truly submersion-proof suit and just really good raingear. But after more than a thousand miles worth of rips and tears from logging slash, berry bushes, barnacles, and rocks, our

A heavy rain sends waterfalls pouring from a cliff in Southeast Alaska's rainforest.

dry suits were no longer dry. In Wrangell, their replacements—a slightly updated version of the original suits—arrived in the mail. In this cold, wet world, fleece was our blubber and the dry suits were our hide. We had become waterproof again.

Distant islands were silhouetted against the sky in varying shades of grey. Fog and rain obscured all but the nearest of them. Raindrops pockmarked the surface of the ocean, forming tiny clear marbles that rolled down the face of each wave. Cascades of water fell in front of me when I shook my head, beading up on the shiny fabric of my brand-new dry suit hood. Our lemon-yellow packrafts were the brightest things in the entire blue-grey world.

It was the time of year when the rainforest earns its name. Tea-brown creeks rushed over their banks, pouring in waterfalls over the edges of sea cliffs and spattering on the rocks below. Beads of water hung on the leaves of every bush.

As the rain rolled off my slick blue coat, I tried to let the calm of the soft grey world soak into me. The drops came hard, bouncing white off the calm grey ocean, blurring the waves into ghosts. And as I watched the ripples spread, I tried to make peace with the rain—to become a rainforest creature myself.

· · ·

We woke to red squirrels, pelting us with what seemed to be their entire winter store of spruce cones as we cooked breakfast under the trees. About twenty-five miles north of the town of Petersburg, we were camped on the shores of Farragut Bay. Across the bay, we watched the white plumes of spouting humpback whales. We laughed at the sea lions. And we hungered after the crabs.

Six feet down in perfectly clear water, fat Dungeness crabs crawled across the sandy bottom. In the best spots, I could peer over the side of my packraft and see five at once. Hig explained to me that as a child he used to attach a net to a long pole and dangle it over the side of a boat. The crabs would get angry and attack the net, tangling their claws, allowing them to be pulled aboard. Perhaps as a child, he had a boat less prone to spinning in circles at the slightest touch. Or a net better than an empty backpack. Whatever the difference, these crabs were never more than mildly annoyed when Hig poked them. He twisted and bent over the side of the packraft, probing the water, while sea lions performed a strange and complex dance behind us.

As we paddled north, sea lions were becoming more and more common. They traveled the coast in packs, swimming in tight formation, almost on top of one another. Upon seeing us, they reared out of the water for a better look, slippery brown torsos leaning together like the singers in a barbershop quartet. Then they dove in unison, each sea lion turning in a graceful arc toward the outside edge of the circle. They formed a fountain of animals, disappearing in a giant coordinated splash like a group of synchronized swimmers, only to pop up again a few feet away and repeat the process.

But as we climbed the wooded hillside above Farragut Bay, the marine wildlife disappeared again behind a curtain of trees. It was a mostly dry day, but each step through the thick understory of blueberry bushes let loose a shower of saved-up rain.

Hig spoke from the bushes behind me: "I'm tired of the Inside Passage. I'm still enjoying it, but I just feel that some of the sense of exploration is gone. I kind of get the Inside Passage now. I know what to expect."

"Yeah, I know what you mean," I said, kicking to untangle my feet from a particularly reluctant branch.

Our days and weeks had fallen into a predictable pattern. We paddled forested shores, made short land crossings across thickly forested islands and headlands, and then returned to the packrafts. The challenges had become familiar, and although the landscape and wildlife still delighted us, they rarely surprised us. As much as we loved the rainforest, the perpetual sogginess of a dark grey September had begun to wear us down.

• • •

Over the pass from Farragut Bay, we descended through the forest to Sandborn Canal, inflating our packrafts in the fields of brown beach grass along the rocky shore. It was the beginning of Dungeness crab and shrimp season, and as we paddled out into the bay, we saw six fishing boats anchored in the middle of it.

"Where's the rest of your boat!?!" Elbows on the rail, beer in hand, the fisherman hollered to us from the stern of his boat.

Bobbing slightly up and down in the gentle chop, we looked up at the four shrimp fishermen who were looking very confusedly down at us.

"We've come from Seattle…," Hig began.

"And we're headed out to the first Aleutian Island…," I continued.

"We walk, and we paddle these little boats…"

"They only weigh five pounds, and we can carry them over the mountains, like that pass back there." I gestured toward the forested hills at the head of the bay.

The self-titled "Wrangell Boys" were drinking a few beers while they let their shrimp pots soak, and we spent several entertaining minutes hearing about all the ways they thought we might die.

"No way you came from Seattle in those things. I would only go in one of them things if the boat sank! What do you do if you get a hole in your boat?"

"Patch it," Hig replied simply. "What do you do if you get a hole in *your* boat?"

The fisherman tapped the steel hull: "I don't get holes."

"Same for us. We don't get holes either."

They proceeded to tell us how we should be carrying a gun for the bears and a VHF radio for the weather, drunkenly talking over us as we tried to explain our choices and precautions.

One guy was fixated on the tides. "You got to divide your tide into twelves. And you got your first hour. That's hour one…"

Another fisherman broke in. "Do you know it takes an expert to tell the difference between the skull of a sea lion and the skull of a brown bear?"

The first fisherman continued: "…One. Two. Three. And your strongest current is on three. In the third hour…"

A third man broke in: "You guys are going to get eaten by orca whales!"

We gave up trying to explain our cautious approach to wilderness hazards, nodding and smiling at the rest of their warnings as we pushed off to paddle toward Port Houghton.

"They probably wouldn't have bothered us if I had told them I'd grown up in Alaska and that my father had fished for eighteen years," Hig grumbled. "Not that it actually has anything to do with this trip."

"I'm sure that we've spent more time in brown-bear country than any of them."

As we were leaving Sandborn Canal, sunspots were shifting around the bay in Port Houghton beyond. Patches of light danced over the land, and the trees and moss glowed green-gold against the dark blues and grey of the sky. A rainbow touched down at the end of a narrow point, the red and blue bands split by the top of a solitary spruce tree.

"You know," Hig began, "those fishermen back there...they're like a lot of people we meet—they think we might die. They're not sure if we're going to survive this. It doesn't make sense, but it makes me not quite so sure either...."

"But they're ridiculous. They think we're going to get eaten by orca whales! And the people we've interacted with for longer—they don't think like that."

"I know. It's just these short encounters, and it doesn't mean anything. But psychologically, it adds a weight."

"You know, if we die, the newspapers are all going to talk about how we didn't have enough stuff, or the right experience, or that we were reckless... I'll fall off a cliff and they'll say we should have had a VHF radio."

I've always thought of myself as a cautious person, even to the point of being cowardly at times. And we had a hard time reconciling our own self-images with how everyone else seemed to view us. In one interview, we were asked to rate ourselves between one and ten on a risk-taking scale. I gave myself a four and Hig chose a five, while the interviewer placed us at eight or nine. People we talked to imagined the whole journey at once—and many seemed to see it as one gigantic 4,000-mile-long hazard. But hazards came one at a time. While we had to be prepared for swirling windstorms, pounding rain, whiteouts, extreme cold, bears, waves, cliffs, difficult navigation, and a shortage of food, we never encountered all of them simultaneously. On most days, we had nothing to worry about at all.

. . .

On the far side of Port Houghton, we pulled ashore to camp just before the start of another expanse of clear cuts. Though we hadn't realized it until hundreds of miles later, somewhere in the Great Bear Rainforest we had crossed another boundary. We were beyond the second-growth logging. The farther north we traveled, the slower the forests grew. Our host in Wrangell had described the spindly forests just behind town: Cut by the Russians in the 1800s, the trees still hadn't grown large enough to be profitably cut again. Well over a hundred years old, the forest was still immature. And most of the second growth in the Tongass was far younger.

On the scale of human industry, logging in Southeast Alaska is a one-time, unsustainable operation—strip-mining the trees. The realization surprised me. Absent a few of the more southern tree species, the rainfor-ests here looked like the rainforests we'd seen on the start of our journey in Washington and southern British Columbia. Walking through these north-ern forests, I couldn't see how much slower they grew. Here the problem wasn't just that sustainable logging wasn't practiced. On anything but the smallest of scales, it was impossible.

It began to seem as silly to grow wood pulp in Alaska as it would be to grow oranges. And about as economical. We sell these trees at a loss. The Forest Service heavily subsidizes logging in the Tongass, largely through building roads for the developers. Since 1980, taxpayers have shelled out nearly a billion dollars in these subsidies, paying private companies to log public trees.

. . .

The following night, having passed beyond the clear cuts, we camped on a bed of brown needles on a point of land extending into Stephens Passage. A dark grove of young spruce and hemlock encircled us.

"Do you hear that?" Hig asked, prodding me awake in depths of our sleeping bag cocoon.

"Mmmm?" I sleepily pulled back the hood I was wearing so I could hear better.

No need. A long, low tone was followed by an eerie trumpeting squeal, then the abrupt *"psssht!"* of an explosive breath.

"I think it's whales!"

We listened in silence as further ghostly songs drifted in from the sea—certain now that we were hearing whales. Blasts from hoarse trombones were followed by long squeaks, erupting spouts, and an occasional *"gaaawooosh!"* The whales sounded so clear and close in the still dark night that I was sure they were in the forest with us. As I drifted off to sleep again, the whales kept singing. Every time I woke, I could hear them— filling the still night air with their eerie lullabies.

As we paddled north the next day, the whales—which we now knew were humpbacks—cruised up and down Stephens Passage, feeding in the rich currents off every point. White columns of whale breath surrounded us. They were almost as noisy during the day as they had been at night, bantering back and forth in a companionable chatter of honks and squeals, punctuated by the explosive sound of spouts. Their rounded backs and tiny dorsal fins arced barely above the water as they came up to breathe, followed by the occasional graceful flash of a tail.

"I wish they were closer," I lamented.

"They seem to be cruising back and forth just off the point here," Hig pointed out. "If we paddled out a ways, they might come right toward us. We'd be fighting the current though."

"I don't know. Maybe let's paddle out just a little bit, to see."

But as soon as we got there, it seemed as though all the whales had become far away spouts again.

"We are fighting quite a bit of current out here."

"I know," I acknowledged sadly, turning back toward shore.

But just as we'd found with Knight Inlet's porpoises, the curiosity was mutual.

I'm not sure if I heard or saw or felt it first, but suddenly, it was there. Twenty feet from my packraft, a rounded back rose gently above the waves.

"Oh my god," I exclaimed in a whisper.

I imagined the big whale eye, just underwater, peering at my tiny yellow raft.

That night, I wrote in my journal under a sky full of stars, every few words punctuated by the breath of a whale. I put down my pencil, listening to the harmony of whale songs and spouts, the steady rumble of a boat motoring down Stephens Passage, and the soft and rhythmic breathing of Hig sleeping beside me.

. . .

We walked the Glass Peninsula, a narrow finger of land running along the east side of Admiralty Island between Stephens Passage and Seymour Canal. Beneath the forest canopy, with the extra exertion of walking, the chill autumn breeze didn't feel as cutting as it did on the water. We followed well-worn bear trails through the open understory, through pale-yellow blueberry bushes that were quickly fading to brown. Each time Hig bent a branch along the trail ahead of me, a rain of small yellow leaves would fall behind him. Hedgehog and angel's wing mushrooms sprouted from the forest floor in amazing profusion, and I collected more than we could possibly fit in our pot for dinner. Crossing the peninsula through a low muskeg pass, we squelched through the bright-orange grasses and dark-red sphagnum moss that grew between the twisted pines.

Admiralty Island is a national monument—one of the few protected lowland forests in the Tongass. Its claim to fame is hosting the densest concentration of brown (grizzly) bears on the planet. Craters lined with scattered and broken leaves showed where the island's famous inhabitants had been digging for skunk cabbage roots. Long-decayed salmon remains—bear food from another season—lined the banks of even the smallest streams.

At night, we left the trails and beaches to the bears, to camp on the peninsula's windswept rocky points. We were getting closer to Glacier Bay. For dozens of miles around that long fiord, the world is rising. In the past two centuries, the bay's vast glacier has retreated and the land has begun to rebound—nearly an inch a year—as it is liberated from the weight of the ice. On the points, sea cliffs stand abandoned, now far above high tide and creating perfect campsites in their lees. We slept beneath the branches of crab apple and maple trees, their hot, dense wood fueling blazing campfires.

Fall had arrived. We could feel it in the chill breeze, see it in the yellowing leaves—even smell it. Change was in the air. Surprises were popping up daily. And our sense of excitement had returned.

• • •

As we lay cozily under our pyramid shelter, the wind came up howling. Peering through the flap on the door, we could see Seymour Canal churning in white foam. Every tiny plant on Admiralty Island was bent and folded downwind, quaking in the gusts. The trees were whipping in the wind even on the forest trails, and as we walked, we watched the whitecaps from the relative comfort of the beaches.

Leaving Wrangell, we had worried about these fall winds. We'd been nervous about being stranded on shore, on the wrong side of one of many inlets we needed to cross. But fall had proved more rainy than stormy, and as travel continued to be kind to us, our thinking had changed. In this land of dense forests, paddling was nearly always faster than walking. So whenever possible, we paddled—exploring the coastline, but missing out on the land.

As October arrived, we found ourselves wishing for a storm. A storm would give us an excuse to walk. It would give us a reason to be smug about being packrafters, walking above the reach of the waves—boats neatly rolled in our packs as we laughed at the weather. And we wanted to see this land exciting and alive in the way only a storm can bring.

The first day, we walked cobble beaches and forest trails, while every tree and bush quaked beneath the force of the wind. But it only lasted a day. By the next morning, the storm had calmed enough for a return to the water. Our supplies had dwindled, we were eager to get to Juneau, and with the packrafts, we could cover miles quickly. Seated in our tiny boats, we ran with the tailwind, surfing the waves, bundled up against the chill in the air. The larger waves broke underneath the rafts, and we surfed their foamy crests.

As we paddled across one small bay, a crab boat motored over to us. "I've been looking for you guys!"

I wrinkled my face in confusion, wondering if someone could possibly have been worried about our whereabouts. We paddled against the wind for a minute, trying to keep alongside the boat, but it was impossible. We grabbed its rails and hung on, riding up and down with every wave, our packrafts whacking the side of the boat.

"You guys have sure got balls!" the fisherman exclaimed. "Or at least one of you has…." His voice trailed off as he awkwardly applied his compliment to a woman. "I've been wondering if I would run into you guys. But I thought you'd be coming up the other side of the peninsula, so I thought I wouldn't. I was just reading your Ketchikan to Wrangell post. I've flown a lot over that country. Here—I was planning to do this on your website."

He handed us two folded bills. Hig grabbed them, keeping a tight grip on the boat's rails with his other hand.

After we thanked him, we talked for a few more minutes, learning about the difficulties of running a crab boat alone and sharing our own recent stories. But the conditions kept our conversation short. A big set of waves set us smacking hard against him, and we pushed off, headed up Seymour Canal with a new glow of pride on our faces. The forty dollars was much appreciated. With that, we could buy over ten pounds of butter! But the positive thought was appreciated even more. We'd had several run-ins with fishing boats on this leg of our journey, and from them we'd been given a pile of delicious Dungeness crabs, some money, and a warning that we were going to die out here. The good encounters outweighed the bad. And the encouragement gave us a newfound energy.

The next day, we walked through the forest again, on our last crossing of Admiralty Island. As we entered one small muskeg patch, Hig interrupted my musings about forest photography in the rain.

"Erin! Look!"

I looked up from the shot I'd been framing to see the back end of a small brown bear, running away across the orange-red sphagnum. I'd just been commenting that we hadn't seen many bears on this trip. It seemed like the crowning moment of a leg that had turned out so much better than we had expected.

7. HOSPITALITY

Our host: "They're such normal, sociable
people. I'm impressed."

THE RAIN WAS UNRELENTING. I stripped off my rain mitts, pouring out the pools of water inside. I took off my fleece gloves, wringing what seemed like a pint of muddy brown water from each. I put them all back on again, only to feel the sopping wet creeping in almost as fast as I'd removed it. My fingers chilled into useless sausages surrounded by soggy insulation. Even in new dry suits, water eventually squirmed in through leak points in my cuffs, running down toward my elbows. It seeped in to soak my butt, making my packraft feel like a chilly bathtub.

It doesn't take a whole lot of energy to reach a packraft's maximum speed. In good conditions, this ease is a blessing. But if something doesn't take much energy, it's hard to keep warm doing it. I gave up on my frozen hands, molding them around the paddle shaft, willing Juneau to be closer.

On a remote coast, I would have shrugged off the downpour. But we were passing the outskirts of Juneau. Each building glowed; windows of lit gold shining over the water as dusk fell on the channel. Each golden square was a spot of warm light in the growing darkness. Each one was a portal to a dry warm place where people sat in luxurious comfort, cozily contemplating the rain outside. Each one taunted me.

As I stood up, dragging my packraft on shore in an empty parking lot, the cooled blood from my stationary legs suddenly circulated through

High tide flattened this beach grass along a channel near Juneau, Alaska.

the rest of my body—sending a shivery chill through my core. Headlights zipped by on the nearby highway. It had been ten days since we had last been indoors.

Packs bulging with poorly arranged gear, packrafts haphazardly strapped on the top, we stumbled through the door of Bullwinkle's Pizza. The tops of our sodden dry suits bulged awkwardly, stretched over the modified sleeping pads we were wearing as life vests and the camera gear we'd stuffed next to our skin to keep it dry and warm. Dripping, dumbfounded by the pizza menu, we eventually managed to order. We had a place to stay in Juneau and a phone number written on a page of waterproof journal paper. But before we could handle actual human interaction over the phone, we needed to become human ourselves.

A football game was blaring on the giant flat screen TV, and as we snacked on pizza, we tried to puzzle out the rules of the game, which neither of us really knew. I felt like an alien species, visiting this strange indoor world.

Our friend Joseph had only one real question for us on the phone: "I just want to ask: Do you really *have* to walk?"

"Yep, we really have to walk," I confirmed, getting detailed directions to his place—three miles away.

Joseph showed up to walk the last piece of Juneau streets with us. Welcoming us inside, he offered showers, clean clothes, and a dinner of salmon and big bowls of stew. We didn't mention that we'd just eaten pizza—we happily devoured the second dinner as well.

Joseph and Eve were kayakers. We'd met Joseph on the Internet months before we'd even begun our trip, emailing back and forth about potential routes through his paddling grounds of Southeast Alaska. And on the strength of that virtual connection, they put us up for five days in their Juneau home. We shared meals and conversation, staying up late talking about tucked-in coves, wave-beaten cliffs, and the paddle routes between.

We had become champion couch crashers. From city apartments to wilderness homesteads, suburban trailers, village houses, and remote work camps—settlements both native and western—we found patches of floor, spare beds, and hospitality. We left piles of wet and dirty gear in their

entryways, sand in their showers, and huge dents in their pantries. We
made new friends.

It started out as the practical solution for a pair of cheapskate hikers.
Sleeping indoors is nice every once in a while. Hotels are expensive, and in
smaller villages, nonexistent. And it's *really* nice to talk to someone besides
your husband every once in a while.

But as we moved through Alaska, we found more and more homes
and lives open to us. The thing we did while we passed through towns and
villages became a reason to go to towns and villages. Sometimes we stayed
with friends of acquaintances, or acquaintances of newly made friends. We
stayed with people we met on the Internet, and people we ran into on the
street. We drew on a circle of connections that broadened as we traveled,
lining up hosts in nearly every outpost we visited. Leaving Seattle, we'd left
our old friends behind. But when we weren't in the wilderness, we never
lacked for company. Joseph and Eve were two new friends out of many.

• • •

Moving west from Juneau, we picked up the faint remains of a trail in the
muskegs of Admiralty Island, discussing the wisdom of a late evening crossing of Lynn Canal. On the west side of the island, the protected nook of
Funter Bay faces out into the five-mile-wide canal. Approaching the water,
we started to pick out the outlines of buildings through the trees and heard
the faint strains of conversation drifting toward us.

"Let's go say hi," Hig suggested.

"I don't know…," I hedged. "This is probably private property."

We were both right. At the edge of a fenced-in garden, we were greeted
by a cacophony of overexcited barking from two little dogs, and a woman
wearing gardening gloves and rubber boots.

"Was that you I just heard on the radio?" she asked. "I was going to
send an email to your website—to invite you to stop by."

"Oh. Yes. Thanks. Well, we wouldn't have gotten it anyway—once we
left town," I explained.

"But here we are," Hig finished, easily accepting Donna and Phil's offer
of dinner and a place to stay for the night.

As we ate a dinner of salmon Phil had caught, we talked about toads.

"Used to be, when you went out to the outhouse at night, there were so many it was hard not to step on them!" Phil reminisced. "But in the thirty-five years I've lived here, they've just about disappeared."

"I think we last saw one three years ago," Donna chimed in.

I racked my brains for our own last sighting of toads—a few weeks ago on the Iskut River, nearly 200 miles away. And I remembered the words of a former homesteader from another Southeast Alaska island: "I'm not sure if my kids have ever seen a toad."

Over the past several decades, western toads have been in dramatic decline across their range, even in these remote reaches of Southeast Alaska. There are many suspected culprits. As glacial rebound pushes the land higher, some of the ponds the toads once bred in are drying up. Warmer winters may stress them. And fungal infections can plague both embryos and adults—infections potentially exacerbated by global warming. These infections have devastated toads in other places, but no one knows how prevalent they are here. There is little research on the toad's decline in Alaska. Much of what we know comes from the observations of long-term residents like Phil and Donna.

The toads weren't the only thing disappearing from Funter Bay. No new yellow cedars were coming up beside the old ones. We wondered what else was changing. In one walk-through of this vast region, we couldn't begin to match the knowledge of lifetimes and generations. Our observations were snapshots in a shifting world. But we tried to be watchers.

· · ·

Our reputation preceded us. On the shore of Excursion Inlet, one notch east of Glacier Bay, a grizzled man waited to greet us. Leaning on his walking stick at the edge of the beach, dressed in blue chest waders, with a long white beard and a mess of wild white hair, "One-Eyed Bob" looked like some kind of remote Alaskan version of Santa Claus.

"I was looking for you guys two days ago!" he called, gesturing to the sign behind him. Scrawled with a marker and tacked to a piece of plywood, it read:

WELCOME TREKKERS
FREE LEMONADE
ALL YOU CAN DRINK
COME ON IN AND REST A WHILE

We had no idea that anyone lived here, but Bob had heard through friends of our impending arrival. We left our packrafts at the top of the beach and followed him to his two small cabins. "I've got showers, and there's water on the stove if you want tea. And you can sleep on the floor of the bathhouse here if you want. I can move these totes out of the way in no time." He shoved aside a plastic fish tote full of clothes.

Bob's one-room cabin was tiny—composed of a table, a bed, a pantry, a gun collection, and the steel stove Bob had welded himself. He showed off his .50 caliber pistol and elephant gun to Hig, and demonstrated how his floor was so tough he could split wood right on it. He'd built it from the salvaged decking of an abandoned cannery. Then he pulled a shiny case from underneath his bed, snapped open the unlocked combination locks, and pulled out a new-looking laptop computer.

"You gotta see this!" he told us excitedly, plugging his laptop into the power from his diesel generator and queuing up a downloaded video. Turning the screen so we could see it, he proudly showed us a car dealership commercial featuring the "Trunk Monkey." Here on this remote and road-less inlet, Bob was showing us a car dealership commercial. The commercial itself was funny. But the reach of modern day advertising was hilarious.

Over a meal of scrambled eggs, Bob told us stories from his adventurous life: how on a boat called *Tuff Enuf*, he had sailed alone through the biggest southeast Pacific hurricane ever recorded; how he'd motorcycled through the southeastern United States; and how he'd worked and lived all across Alaska, doing all kinds of jobs.

It was an Alaskan's story. Alaska is full of fishermen turned professors, physicists turned fishermen, hunting guides turned politicians, and folks who piece together bits and pieces of whatever jobs will let them live, wander, and play in this great state.

Hig had always been an Alaskan. And I was becoming one. The more Alaskans we met, the more I felt as though I belonged among this bizarre mishmash of oddballs and adventurous spirits. Ever since our first journeys together, Hig and I had toyed with the idea of moving north someday. Now, with no commitments beyond this journey, we were increasingly certain that "someday" was at hand. We would find some way to stay.

• • •

Between Excursion Inlet and Gustavus, there was barely a day's travel. We walked under drizzling skies on a beach littered with shells, stabbing them with the tips of our ice axes as we walked by.

"Got the one you missed!"

"These cockle shells are tough! I can hardly get through them!"

The shell-stabbing game was one we'd invented years before, as a way to pass time on long beach walks. As we stabbed, we chattered about the different kinds of shells and speculated about who we might meet in Gustavus.

Each time we met someone, we learned something about their life. And each time we met someone, we re-answered a million similar questions about our own: How can you stand to be together for so much time? What do you talk about all day?

Scientists that we were, we sometimes spent hours in geeky discussions—about the evolution of photosynthesis, or the prediction of tides—trading off teaching each other anything we could ever remember once learning. But as we traveled, much of our conversation was a simple list of banal observations: "Look at that tree." "Lots of skunk cabbage." "Ripe blueberries." "Oops, not a stable log." "A few big barnacles—entirely covered with tiny ones." "Salmon jumped."

Sometimes we would call attention to something rare, unexpected, or especially amazing. But we spent a lot of time stating the obvious. Most of the time, we weren't even pointing it out. I was sure that Hig noticed the barnacles we were paddling past. He was sure that I'd seen giant cedars towering overhead. But those few words served to reaffirm the experience we were having—taking the connection we each felt to the world around us and sharing it with each other.

. . .

On our way out of the small town of Gustavus, on the shores of Glacier Bay, we had one last social dinner. We were about to set out for the Lost Coast—which promised to be far less peopled and far more harsh than this friendly corner of Southeast Alaska. We met up with a friend who'd journeyed with us for a few days out of Ketchikan—the only person to have walked with us since the trails of Seattle. We had pizza and beer with him and a half dozen other interesting people, answering questions about our trip as we gleaned intelligence from them on the section of coast we were about to traverse. Several of them had walked a big chunk of it before, and we pored over maps, learning what little we could in advance.

Heading up the stairs to a fluffy and comfortable guest bed, we overheard our host remarking: "They're such normal, sociable people. I'm impressed."

Hig and I shared a private laugh—chalking our "normalcy" up to low expectations.

Who do people expect us to be?

8. INTO THE STORMS

Erin: "I have never felt so intrepid.
And I have never been so incredibly sandy."

BROWN LUMPS SPECKLED the shores of the narrow gravel island at the mouth of Glacier Bay. We squinted. But the cacophonous grunting, bellowing, and roaring soon left no doubt as to what we were seeing. The island wasn't composed of gravel. It was composed of sea lions.

Crowded onto the same small patch of highly prized beach, the sea lions argued constantly, waving their massive necks from side to side, roaring in the faces of their rivals, waddling forward and backward on the ungainly flippers that seemed unlikely appendages for supporting such massive, blubbery bodies. Sea otters bobbed in the kelp beside us, the first we'd seen all journey. A flock of cormorants wheeled overhead. As we floated past with the tide, Hig pulled out the video camera and began to film.

Perhaps they liked cameras.

A hundred sea lions reared up, all heads pointed toward us. A hundred sea lions charged down the beach, splashing into the water in an awkward rush that was faster than seemed possible. A hundred sea lions started swimming right toward us.

Their brown heads protruded from the water, pink mouths gaping wide with rows of sharp white teeth, letting out their honking guttural roars. They surrounded us in a great wall, a quickly contracting semi-circle

Surf crashes against boulders on the Lost Coast.

of bellowing brown flesh and churning water. The head of one large bull seemed larger than my entire boat.

"*Sea lions eat fish. Sea lions don't eat people. Sea lions eat fish.*"

Those were the words playing in my mind as the wall closed in—a hundred feet, fifty feet, thirty feet…

I briefly tried to paddle away, before realizing there was no way we could outrun a hundred sea lions. We put down the paddles and picked up our cameras. Twenty feet away…

And suddenly, they dove. In one giant choreographed splash, our encircling wall of sea lions was replaced by rippling, grey-blue water.

Backing off underwater, they reappeared, repeating their encroaching circle. Each time, they approached only to twenty feet. Sea lion faces are inscrutable, and it was impossible to tell if they were trying to drive us away or just wanted to play. The group slowly dwindled, but some of them followed us for half an hour. No longer terrified, we were free to be simply amazed.

• • •

As fall descended on us, we spent more and more time in the dark. Each day, our light shrank a little further, and our eight hours of daylight and twilight became ever more precious. When the skies were clear, we often woke under the light of the moon or the stars, shivering against the cold-frosted air as we broke the darkness with a fire. And when clouds blotted out the glittering sky, darkness crept up on us.

One long evening in late October, we watched the landscape fade, only fuzzy outlines of the bear and wolf tracks still visible as black shadows on the dark grey sand. We were left on a black beach under the black heavens above, nothing separating sand from sky. Ocean waves approached from the left, coming in as vague dark lines that suddenly broke, hissing as they crumpled into a dim white. Bright patches of ghostly sea foam blew past our feet, making it seem as though the ground itself was blowing.

As surroundings disappeared, our minds strayed from our formless world, and our conversation leapt thousands of miles away. Is China the oldest nation? What exactly happened with the fall of Soviet communism? How do bombs work?

Even when walking in the dark is physically easy, psychologically it's hard. The sound of the ocean was still with us, as was the feel of the sand underfoot, but much of what makes the world interesting was shrouded and hidden from our diurnal eyes.

We had entered the remote expanse of the Lost Coast, where over 600 miles of travel would be broken by only one town—Yakutat. We were hoping to make the whole distance in a month of traveling, with Yakutat our only resupply point. To meet that goal, we would have to walk more than twenty miles a day. So far on the journey, we'd only managed to average fourteen-and-a-half miles in a day. With each day, the darkness lengthened, making long days of walking more and more difficult. With each day we walked further into darkness and cold.

. . .

At Glacier Bay, we had reached the end of the Inside Passage. Suddenly, there were no more little islands. Suddenly, we were no longer in a complicated maze of protected waterways. We looked southwest across the vast Pacific Ocean, with nothing between us and Hawaii. Nothing between us and the brunt of the weather.

It's hard to describe the Lost Coast in anything but extremes. Giant peaks of the St. Elias Range rise almost straight from the ocean, creating some of the highest relief in the world. Flowing down from their snowy ice fields, North America's largest glaciers spill onto the beach plain in huge, rapidly melting lobes. Storms whipped up in the Aleutians whirl down the coastline, funneled onto the narrow strip of beaches between the roiling ocean and the towering peaks.

Compared to these raw shores, the Inside Passage felt like a much smaller world, defined by islands and enclosed by the rainforest. Out here, everything was open, and the weather was the fabric of the world.

We'd prepared ourselves for the rains of the Lost Coast. Before we left Seattle, I had looked up historical statistics on weather patterns, reading about average temperatures and precipitation for every town along our route. Yakutat quickly jumped out: twenty inches of rain in October! That was even rainier than the rainforest we'd just left. As fall progressed, we quoted the statistic back and forth to each other, trying to prepare ourselves for the inevitable sogginess.

But we had underestimated the Lost Coast's weather. We had underestimated its fickle changeability, its overwhelming power, the constant tension of waiting for the next gust. And we had underestimated the excitement, the intensity, and the wild aliveness the swirling storms could bring. It was terrible. It was all-consuming. And it was the most awesome thing in the world.

We didn't just get rain. We got Weather.

10/22/07: Squalls of pouring rain alternated with spots of brilliant sun. One minute the surface of the lake was glinting with the reflection of brilliant icebergs, the next minute roughened by the heavy patter of bouncing raindrops.

10/23/07: We woke to a thick frost on the ground—icing our shelter, our shoes, the strings staking out our shelter. Dancing tiptoe on a frozen beach like a graceless ballerina, I tried to melt my shoes into foot shapes again as I licked the joints of my frozen kayak paddle.

10/24/07: We woke up to wind. A gust pulled a tie out of our shelter and set the whole thing to a deafening flapping in the pre-dawn moonlight....The north wind has brought us sun, but also some dramatic rain squalls—sideways drops stinging as they pelted us in the face, everything drying almost at once in the cold wind.

10/25/07: The sun appeared, lighting the curls of the waves a turquoise blue, glinting white on the spray blowing off their tops, a blinding white froth as they crashed to shore.

10/27/07: Hard rain and sleet began to fall as we were packing, pounding down and leaving great two-inch-deep pools on the raft we'd been sleeping on, slushy white pellets melting into ice-cold water.

10/30/07: Sea foam bulldozed in with the waves, lying in jiggling heaps on the beach. Caught by a gust, chunks would tear off and fly up the beach, tumbling into hot dogs that left streaky white trails as they flew. A sea duck hid from the storm behind a driftwood log, letting us stand feet away for several seconds before taking

off into the windy surf. Beyond the yellow-orange beach grass, the world disap-
peared into the mist.

10/31/07: We held on tight to the paddles as we crossed a desolate plain of gravel
toward Dry Bay. The wind tugged at my packraft, gusting up from behind, and
I wrapped my arms through the strings, picturing a yellow raft tumbling end
over end in the wind. Sunspots passed over us, creating a brilliant scene of bright-
orange grass and a glowing rainbow against an ominous blue-black sky. Squalls
blew in our faces as we crossed Dry Bay, sending us paddling into torrential hail.
I cinched my hood until there was only the narrowest opening to see through, and
the hailstones beat a deafening drumbeat over my ears.

And that was all before our first big storm.

. . .

We woke to wind again. It tugged and pulled on the nylon panels that
comprised our pyramid shelter, threatening to pull out the buried sticks that
anchored it. With only a leafless alder shrub for a windbreak, we'd banked
sand up against the base of each fluttering wall, trying to stabilize our home
on a field of windblown dunes.

It grew windier. Tucked into our packrafts, we flew down the Akwe
River. Swans and ducks bobbed on the current, letting us drift close, hesi-
tant to fly into the gale. We were blown into shallows almost invisible under
the whipped brown water.

It blew harder. The wind tore swirls of wet sand from the beach. We
draped our deflated rafts over our packs as both windbreaks and sails. Even
on foot, we flew with the wind.

Waves whipped across the breadth of the Italio River, stirring up whitecaps in barely twenty yards of fetch. Blowing sand caked our ankles. Even
deflated, our packrafts jerked and twisted in the gale, and I wondered how
we would ever get across without the balloon-like boats taking to the skies.

I planted one foot in each boat, hunched over and squinting against
the sand blowing in my eyes, while I willed myself to be heavy. Hig held the
inflation bag open, letting the rush of wind fill the rafts with air. Normally
it requires a rhythmic fill-and-push motion to inflate them, but in these

conditions, the bag simply had to funnel the wind. A rime of wet sand buried our packs and paddles beside us. Once launched, we zipped across the river, bucking the strange, choppy waves running perpendicular to the current.

And the storm grew. We hurriedly deflated the rafts, tying them again as wind and sand shields against our backs. The sand was flowing in rivers along the beach, obscuring our tracks almost as soon as we made them. The sand blew higher, no longer limited to a few inches above the ground. We could barely turn our heads an inch without sending stinging wet sand grains against our cheeks and into our eyes. We didn't turn upwind at all anymore. We could only move forwards.

We staggered with the wind along a long, sandy spit that ran parallel to the coastline. One branch of the Italio River lay behind us. In front of us, somewhere, was another branch. To our left, huge waves curled and smashed on the slate-grey sea, whipped into a furious froth. To our right, a lagoon, churning with whitecaps, yawned between our sand spit and the forests and mountains beyond.

As we walked farther out the spit, less and less vegetation grew. Only a few tufts of battered yellow beach grass stood against the world of blowing sand. Rain blew at our backs, but in the pelting of wet sand and the howling wind, we hardly even noticed. I fruitlessly tried to brush off the quarter-inch of sand that had caked on the backs of my arms. We watched the swirls build sandcastles on the upwind side of every piece of driftwood, and let the wind push our bodies and legs downwind like a novice puppet master.

I'd never seen wind strong enough to throw *wet* sand into the air. This wind had started doing that hours ago and had only increased since then. The storm was exhilarating—alive. I wanted to keep flying with the wind. But I knew we were trapping ourselves. Since our crossing of the Italio, the wind had grown by leaps and bounds. Another packraft crossing, however short, wouldn't be safe to even try. And with water on all four sides, this sand spit was a solid dead end, right in the brunt of the storm.

It was about the size of an SUV—a small dune, sporting a smaller patch of sparse, half-buried grass on its upwind side. Eddies of sand swirled up on the downwind side, occasionally catching our faces. Neither of us wanted to stop so early. But staring into the flat infinity of beach before us, we knew there was nothing but water beyond. It looked like the last semblance of shelter we were going to get.

With raw cold fingers poking through holes in my gloves, I scrabbled at the sand, unburying a driftwood log. I hoisted it, grunting. Peering at the window of sand between my feet, I tried to retrace my steps as the blowing sand worked to obscure them. It was a struggle to move even my body against the force of the wind, not to mention the heavy log. I stumbled a little, misjudging how far I needed to lean backwards. I didn't dare turn my eyes toward the wind. Finally, back at the jumble of footprints that marked our camp, I laid the log on top of the low wall we were building, chinking the gaps with sand. Awkward and backwards, we built a whole shelter.

My face, my hands, my ears, my nose…even my throat felt gritty. After two hours of slow work, I wriggled into the tiny space we had built. The howling world outside receded, the roar of the wind muffled by the logs, sand, and packrafts that formed our crude shelter. Compared to the deafening scream of the wind outside, the sand pelting our roof seemed almost silent.

There was just enough room for us to both squirm in and bury ourselves in our gear. We didn't take off our dry suits. We didn't even take off our shoes. I was sure that if I unzipped anything in this much sand, I'd never get it closed again. We draped our shelter over us, using it to protect the sleeping bag from wet and sand. Water dripped on our feet as we snuggled close together to stay warm. I wrote in my journal, my cold hand filling the pages with loopy, uncoordinated writing, smearing the waterproof paper with gritty wet sand.

Each time I woke up in the night, I shivered, snuggling even closer to Hig's warmth, and wiggling whichever of my body parts still had room to move. I counted to one hundred as I performed each rhythmic motion—crunching my stomach and flexing my feet—hoping the exercise would warm me up enough for another bout of sleep.

That night the storm gave one last crashing roar and then vanished. I was asleep, but Hig described hearing a terrible roar followed by what sounded like buckets of water hitting the rafts over our heads. Then the wind stopped. The calm was as distinct as the storm that preceded it.

An orange and rising sun hung low over the water the next morning, lighting the remains of the waves. Golden plains of grass glowed against a dark, blue-black sky. We hadn't moved an inch, but we woke up in an entirely different world.

. . .

We staggered into the Yakutat grocery store, overwhelmed by the screaming display of closely packed bright colors and bold slogans. It had been sixteen long days since we had left Gustavus. It was the longest we'd carried our food without running into any generous souls or long-abandoned stashes. It was the longest we'd gone without seeing another human being.

I was desperately hungry. And theoretically, everything I was looking at was food. But none of it was comprehensible. Orange was a plain of beach grass, blue-white the snout of a glacier, pink a swath of garnet sand or ocean sunrise, grey the sweep of ocean waves. Real colors were muted, softly blending into each other on the spacious canvas of open land. The grocery store boxes glowed with a jarring intensity I could hardly recognize.

We stumbled around stupidly for several minutes, enjoying the warmth and brightness, but unable to actually identify and choose any food items. When we eventually wandered out, we clutched heavy bags of bread, oranges, juice, yogurt, and a pint of strawberry ice cream inspired by many days walking hungry through wild strawberry fields long past their season. I shivered as I ate my ice cream on the steps, not even minding the cold.

As best as we could tell, Yakutat was the halfway spot on our entire journey, about 2,000 miles out of the 4,000 we were planning. This 800-person town sits on Yakutat Bay, one of the few tuck-ins on the open shore of the Lost Coast. Known for surfing, fishing, and having a daily jet flight despite its small size, it's the only town in 400 miles of coast—600 miles measured by the winding route we were walking.

And Yakutat adopted us.

We camped out in a little trailer by the school. People delivered groceries, fresh-gathered chanterelle mushrooms, and a couple bottles of beer. Kids brought jars of salmon and moose meat, and a little paper cup with strips of french toast dipped in syrup. We were the empty-handed guests of honor at a potluck, happily stuffing our faces as we shared tales of the trip and heard stories from the locals. We gave a slideshow presentation for the kids in the school, and again for the adults in the evening. We had almost more invitations than we knew what to do with.

When we were finally ready to leave, the whole school was waiting in the hallway, chattering and enjoying the break from class as we rushed in late. It was only a day before Hig's birthday, and the kids sang "Happy Birthday" in front of the Yakutat school sign, where we all posed for pictures. The principal ceremoniously presented Hig with a two-pound block of cheese. It had snowed the night before, one of the first snows of the season. The kids all joined us for the first mile out of town, playing in the snow on the road, the little ones leaving a trail of lost mittens as they ran. And then it was just the two of us again, our feet crunching softly on a thin veneer of melting snow on gravel. Ahead was the second half of the Lost Coast, with three major crossings and the deepening dark of winter.

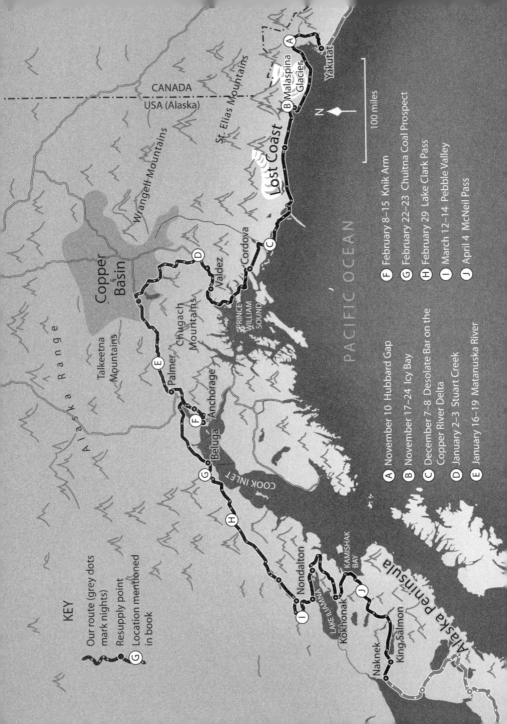

KEY

Our route (grey dots mark nights)

Resupply point

Location mentioned in book ⬤ G

CANADA
USA (Alaska)

St. Elias Mountains

Lost Coast

Wrangell Mountains

Copper Basin

Talkeetna Mountains

Chugach Mountains

Alaska Range

Valdez

Cordova

PRINCE WILLIAM SOUND

Palmer

Anchorage

Beluga

COOK INLET

Nondalton

LAKE ILIAMNA

Kolkhonak

KAMISHAK BAY

Naknek

King Salmon

Alaska Peninsula

PACIFIC OCEAN

Yakutat

Malaspina Glacier

N

100 miles

A November 10 Hubbard Gap
B November 17–24 Icy Bay
C December 7–8 Desolate Bar on the Copper River Delta
D January 2–3 Stuart Creek
E January 16–19 Matanuska River

F February 8–15 Knik Arm
G February 22–23 Chuitna Coal Prospect
H February 29 Lake Clark Pass
I March 12–14 Pebble Valley
J April 4 McNeil Pass

WINTER

[November 8–April 14]

1,407 miles

9. ICE

Erin: "In the daylight,
at least it's a photogenic obstacle."

NEARLY TWENTY MILES WIDE at its mouth, Yakutat Bay is the largest
bite into the expanse of beaches that makes up the Lost Coast. In its upper
reaches, it narrows into Disenchantment Bay. Then it narrows further,
funneling into the Hubbard Gap, a slender notch between Gilbert Point
and the Hubbard Glacier. Gilbert Point is the northern tip of the peninsula that houses the town of Yakutat—jutting in toward the glaciers and
mountains of the St. Elias range. At the head of the bay, the water squeezes
through the Hubbard Gap, then turns south and opens out again, into the
calm, protected waters of Russell Fiord.

Even without the Lost Coast weather, the twenty-mile-wide mouth
of Yakutat Bay was far too long a crossing for our packrafts. We planned
to paddle out Russell Fiord to the Hubbard Gap, scoot through the
constricted, ice-filled channel at the toe of the glacier, then cross Disenchantment Bay at its northern end—only two miles across.

Only the turquoise blue of the calving glacier stood out against the
monochrome world—grey water, grey-brown bushes against stark white
snow, black and white peaks, and the warmer grey of the sky. Active and
unpredictable, Hubbard Glacier was in a constant cycle of surge and retreat,
sometimes blocking off Russell Fiord completely. The face of the ice had

Hig stares across the ice-choked waters of Icy Bay the morning after our first
crossing attempt.

long since plowed over the island our map showed in the middle of the channel, dramatically shrinking the gap of water where icebergs swirled in the strong tidal currents. Only a 300-yard opening remained between the ice of Hubbard Glacier and the rock of Gilbert Point.

Ice swirled in rising tide eddies, concentrating icebergs into shifting lines. Cormorants sat on a turquoise-blue ice block—floating rapidly up the bay. Seagulls wheeled in front of the massive face of the glacier, emphasizing its scale. We had been told that the calving would slow at slack tide. So we waited on the snow-dusted shore, packrafts in hand, listening as slabs of ice cracked and peeled from the miles-long face, collapsing into the water in a nearly constant series of rumbles and booms.

Just before slack tide, we launched. A red and white Cessna screamed past overhead, banking low over the glacier before turning around to zoom even lower over us. I could almost feel the wind from the wings. Then a sudden splash as a ziploc bag fell between the icebergs just in front of me. I unwrapped the good-luck package of trail mix, chocolate, and a flashlight, waving my thanks to the pilot from Yakutat. Two days after we'd left, the town was still watching over us.

On our right, the glacier calved. On our left, pebbles rolled down a steep slope of bare rock, scraped clean from the last time the glacier had plowed into it. Just in front of us, a sea otter floated calmly, seemingly undisturbed by its unstable environs.

I was keyed up and buzzing with adrenaline—ready for monster waves set off by the impacts of calving ice, ready for rolling bergs, ready for the threat of ice closing in around me.

The slack tide we'd been waiting for was just a single moment's pause of gently swirling water. But everything was calm. Our passage felt almost surreal, in a world of smooth grey water and bobbing white ice. We followed the dropping tide current, floating out beyond the Hubbard Gap, and paddling easily to the bay's far shore. One of the Lost Coast's major crossings was behind us. But two more—Icy Bay and the Copper River—still remained.

...

The stream began in a spiraling whorl, bubbling up like a fountain from the top of a set of terraced steps, straight from the muddy floor of the young alder forest. The steps were made of ice. Super-cooled water rushed up from a great depth, freezing as it reached the lower pressure of the surface. Which meant that the brushy patch of alder, devil's club, and salmonberry we'd been walking through was a part of the Malaspina Glacier. Hundreds of feet of ice lay beneath us, stretching far below sea level. We'd been walking past, or on, the Malaspina Glacier for days, but camouflaged beneath its blanket of forest and brush, we might never have noticed the ice.

Nearby, a patch of muddy grass opened onto a small lagoon—a third of a mile wide—ringed all around with bluffs of dirty ice. On top of the ice cliff, a young spruce forest waited for its inevitable demise. Trees leaned precariously over the melting bluff. Carpets of forest soil that had once lain on ice hung over the rapidly melting edge, blowing in the wind. A pile of fresh trees lay in the water below, upturned and broken. At high tide, the surf crashed over the boulders and through the narrow opening, sending streaks of sea foam across the bite-sized lagoon.

On our thirty-year-old maps, this was the Sitkagi Bluffs. The USGS drew cliffs of ice three hundred feet high, running for miles along the shore. But the ice cliff over the lagoon was barely fifty feet tall, and we hadn't seen a hint of a bluff anywhere else. I tried to picture the sheer volume of ice that had melted since the maps were drawn. Hig speculated with a hazard geologist's glee. Perhaps the relatively warm salt water running into the lagoon could set off a catastrophic melting cascade—turning this thirty-five-mile-wide lobe of ice into a giant ocean bay within only a handful of years.

On the Lost Coast, geology was now. The world was building, crumbling, shifting, and melting before our eyes.

And it wasn't just the glaciers that moved. As the lobes of ice retreated, entire rivers disappeared with them. As the powerful storms and currents moved sand along the shore, the mouths of the rivers still remaining shifted miles westward on the coast. As the weight of ice was relieved, the land rose up, sending beaches marching out into what had been the realm of the ocean. In other places, rivers feeding sand to the beach had moved, setting off rapid erosion. Ocean waves curled where forests had stood before.

"Are we *sure* it's not high tide?" I asked, dodging a wave by sprinting up the beach, right to the edge of the trees.

"Of course we're sure," Hig replied, also sprinting. "High tide's not until well after dark."

But the mid-tide waves ran up the beach berm, sloshing sand into our shoes when we couldn't escape them, and spilling into the marshes and willows on the other side. Trees toppled into the surf. Sand poured into the forests, burying sad-looking spruce and willows that had started their lives farther from the ocean. It wasn't long before the eroding beach vanished entirely beneath the tide, sending us thrashing through twisted thickets of alder, wishing for our previously ubiquitous bear trails.

Southeast of Yakutat, the entire Lost Coast had been one giant bear trail. Steep headlands were girded by neat terraces cut by giant paws. Paths were worn into the gravel of the beaches. Huge footprints marked the garnet sand, leaving imprints that stood out magenta-pink against the grey.

But even the bears couldn't keep up with the rapid erosion along the edge of the Malaspina Glacier. And as November wore on, the bears were disappearing into slumber. As we approached the next bite in the coast at Icy Bay, the only tracks we saw were the erratically wandering prints of a lone small cub.

$\cdots$

At Icy Bay, we left the surf-pounded beaches behind, turning inland to follow the curve of the bay. The first thing we saw was a set of four-wheeler tracks. Along the Lost Coast, we'd passed fishing camps closed up for winter, ancient miners' trails, and mysterious rusting machinery. But we hadn't seen a soul outside of Yakutat. What was someone doing in such a remote spot in late November? We traded guesses as we walked up the strangely quiet shore, protected from the brunt of the open coast's surf. A logger? A homesteader?

No. Reality TV.

The Discovery Channel was filming a show called *The Alaska Experiment*. They had stationed four groups of people in cabins and wall tents in remote locations. The participants were supposed to fend for themselves for four months—with a good chunk of provided food, bear guards, and restrictive insurance regulations preventing them from using boats to go fishing.

Between the two groups stationed in Icy Bay (the other two groups were elsewhere in Alaska), the three men on the film crew, the couple that ran the local lodge, and the bear guards and hunting guides, Icy Bay was an insular little world of about fifteen people—all of whom, save us, were under contract with the Discovery Channel.

Their reality was surviving on the protected side of Icy Bay for another month or so. Our reality had to take us across it. We chatted with the lodge owner and the cameraman under the blue light of a rainy dawn, gulping down eggs, bacon, and potatoes before heading up the bay to a narrower crossing point.

Our clothes were dry. The energy of a good rest and warm food filled our bodies. The weather looked manageable, with a stiff breeze, but no obvious storm on the horizon. It seemed as good a day as any to attempt a crossing.

Blowing up our packrafts near a narrow point in Icy Bay, I tore the sleeping pad/life vest I'd been wearing. I wanted to end the attempt right there. Hig calmly pointed out that we might not get decent weather conditions again anytime soon, and that the packraft was the real life saver, not the vest. I reluctantly agreed with his logic. But for some inexplicable reason, it just didn't feel right to cross.

"I don't know, but I have a bad feeling about this crossing—more than for any other crossing we've done," I tried to explain.

Hig replied a little skeptically. "I agree I'd like a little more margin for error, but I think we're doing pretty well."

So we launched. Initially, we made good progress across the bay, driven by a brisk tailwind. I wished the swells and chop were a little smaller, but it was nothing we couldn't handle. But the feeling of trepidation stuck with me—just as strongly as before. I concentrated on turning my boat to align with the largest of the waves, trying to quiet my mind. In the growing dusk, waves broke into ghostly white around me, sending the boat surging toward Icy Bay's western shore.

The glaciers that once filled Icy Bay had shrunk dramatically. But shrunken is not gone, and each finger of the bay still ended in a great calving face of ice, spitting bergs into the ocean as ice flowed down from the peaks. We'd known it was a potential sticking point. We knew of people who had walked this coast before, but all had gotten rides across the major water bodies. And none had come in November.

"That looks like a line of icebergs on the left," Hig pointed out. "If we cross that, it should cut the chop some."

It worked. I started to relax a bit as the chop dissipated and the far shore grew closer. It was raining. Night was falling. I was ready to be on land—imagining fire, dinner, and our cozy sleeping bag.

Then we hit ice. This was no thin line conveniently placed to cut the chop. Quickly it became apparent that there was a solid wall of packed ice between us and the shore. The same wind that had sailed us so quickly across the bay had been blowing the ice—perhaps stacking it up for days— creating an impenetrable quarter mile of crashing bergs between the water and the land. Refrigerator-sized chunks of ice shifted in the swell, ramming together in a grinding crush, breaking into smaller places, and leaving barely a hand's width channel between them.

We turned right, paddling up the bay along the edge of the grinding ice wall, looking for an opening. We were no longer aligned with the wind, and whitecap after whitecap crashed broadside into our rafts. The ice wall couldn't be infinite, but as it stretched farther and farther in the failing light, we discussed the troubling possibility that it might be.

My amorphous bad feeling had solidified into a truly bad reality, but there was no joy in saying "I told you so." I shifted in my pool of ice water, wondering how long we could paddle before we ran out of energy and got too cold. I wondered what would happen if the wind picked up, pushing us irreversibly into the wall of ice. It wasn't hard to imagine an outcome that scared me—it seemed all too easy to disappear in this cold dark world, so far from land.

"If things really go to hell, we get on a berg and flip the EPIRB, OK?" Hig said firmly.

"OK...," I agreed hesitantly, looking at how small the nearest icebergs were. Barely the size of a kitchen table. "If we can find one big enough. But I think we should just follow the edge of this ice. Eventually we'll get to one shore or the other. As long as we can paddle. If we get hypothermic, we might start making bad decisions, so I think we should decide now, and stick to it."

"OK."

Dark fell, slowly shrinking our small grey circle of visibility. No moon or stars could penetrate the rain clouds, and even our well-adjusted eyes could barely see more than grey smudges of ice against the dark water. Immediately to my left, I watched the jagged forms of the iceberg wall, crunching and grinding in the waves. Just ahead of me, I stared at Hig's back—the bright yellow and blue of his packraft faded into monochrome darkness. The thin line of ice we'd been so happy to cross had vanished, and only an occasional ghostly berg passed by on our right, momentarily blocking the chop. All around us, the breaking tips of waves glowed grey against the black sea. Beyond that tiny circle, the wall of ice quickly faded into the distance. Then there was nothing. I could only imagine the land.

The wind held steady. Hig's greater strength gave him an edge, and I paddled in his lee, so close I was nearly bumping his packraft with my bow. We paddled at an angle into the wind, pointing forty-five degrees from our actual trajectory, fighting the gusts that threatened to push us into the ice, and making painfully slow progress that we measured against each passing berg.

Waves occasionally sheeted across the deck of the rafts, adding to the pools inside. It never stopped raining. Our worn-out spray decks were incapable of keeping out so much water for so many hours. We sat in icy baths, water slowly soaking in through all the cracks and crevices of our dry suits—new in Wrangell, but already over 600 miles worn.

I knew we couldn't stop paddling, not even for a moment. We couldn't afford to lose ground. We couldn't afford to lose heat. We both peed in our dry suits, lacking any other option. It felt warm. My fingers were glued to the paddle, insensitive to the cold. The only way out was to keep going.

And we had to keep talking. It would keep us both going. The line of ice had led us back into the middle of the bay. There was no opening, and with every stroke, the west shore, now invisible, shrank farther into the distance behind us. It seemed clear we'd have to fight the wind all the way back to the shore we'd started on.

"I love you!" I yelled.

"I love you too!"

"You're the most awesome person in the world, and we're going to make it to that shore, and it's going to be wonderful!"

"Yes! We're doing great!"

The shore was still invisible. I hoped that a subtle difference in the shadowed sky marked a low, tree-covered moraine rising behind the beach. Fear lingered in the back of my mind, pushed back so I could focus on immediate concerns. I felt cold, but not hypothermic. We were well acclimated to cold and wet. Strengthened by five months of paddling, I felt as though my arms could last forever. And the large breakfast the lodge owner had given us that morning still filled our bodies with energy.

"I was thinking, about our earlier conversation…," Hig said a little later, shouting against the wind. "I think we should have a kid. I don't see a good reason we shouldn't. Maybe even soon after this trip."

It was a bizarrely out-of-place comment that was at the same time perfectly appropriate. We were both focused on our own lives already—why not another?

"I agree," I yelled back, surprising myself a little with the answer as thoughts of a future child ran through my head.

We shouted increasingly wild and silly speculations about our future child back and forth for a while. But eventually, my brain was as tired as the rest of me, and I could no longer think of anything coherent to say.

"ABCDEFG, HIJKLMNOP, QRS, TUV, WX, Y, and Z. Now I know my ABCs! Next time won't you sing with me!" I yelled the alphabet song at the top of my lungs, running through it over and over again with barely a breath between verses, only pausing occasionally to poke fun at myself.

We had left our edge of ice behind, heading into the darkness, straining our ears for the sound of surf on rock—nearly back to the shore we'd launched from, but five miles farther up the bay. Eventually, even over my screaming alphabet song, I could hear the rhythmic hiss of surf. We had no idea how big the waves were, but we knew they would bring us into shore. We surfed smoothly in with the surge, stumbled out awkwardly, and dragged our boats up the beach. It had been five hours of continuous paddling. Our failure of imagination had brought us closer to a "death scenario" than we ever wanted to get.

Safely on shore, I couldn't help thinking about the bad feeling I'd had about the crossing. I *never* had feelings like that. We used logic to make our decisions, not gut instinct. And my gut had never before disagreed. Was it chance? Or did my subconscious know something I didn't? I wasn't sure what to believe, but I knew I wouldn't ignore a feeling like that again.

· · ·

"In the daylight, at least it's a photogenic obstacle," I observed the next morning.

We watched, eating breakfast, as a seemingly continuous line of icebergs flowed out from the upper reaches of Icy Bay. A dusting of snow covered the rocks on our beach. And the blue-white ice stretched as far as we could see.

When storms screamed through, they blew the ice out to sea. When they died, they left a steady southeast wind, packing the ice up against the far shore and preventing any landing. We were stuck waiting for a seemingly impossible happy medium.

On day two, we stared at the impenetrable ice as we wandered up the bay and photographed our dilemma.

On day three, we tied a stout spruce pole to the bottom of both rafts, creating a longboat with a keel that could better fight the wind. We

ventured out, watching the gusts carefully, looking for the wall of ice. Half
a mile from what appeared to be a still impenetrable wall, a large gust
swept past, ruffling the water. Remembering how a storm could begin in an
instant, we beat a hasty retreat. And then, realizing that our food reserves
wouldn't last much longer, we packed up and spent the evening retracing
our steps to the world of reality TV.

On day four, we sat at the lodge, drinking hot chocolate, watching a
storm through the window. The lodge owner displayed his accumulated
beachcombing treasures from a life along the Lost Coast. He even had
a vertebra and tooth from a "sea monster." He showed us a photo of the
strange carcass. It looked like nothing I'd ever seen: a huge mouth full of
long teeth on a finned furry body.

Day five was Thanksgiving. We left the lodge in early morning darkness with a gift of fresh moose meat, hoping for a window to cross the bay.
This time the wind was in our faces. After half an hour of paddling into
an increasing wind, we returned to our now-familiar campsite at the head
of the bay, roasting moose meat over the fire, thankful for our food and
our safety.

On day six, I barely left the tiny confines of our eight-by-eight-foot
shelter, listening to the storm rail outside. The alders we had used for
anchoring the corners whipped in the wind, and we spent the day eating
and dozing to the steady drumbeat of rain on our nylon roof.

On day seven, we woke to quiet. The full moon lit a cloud hanging low
over the upper bay, while stars shone through in dark-blue gaps between
the grey clouds. Dawning light on our "Holdup Cove" lit white streams of
ice in the middle of the bay. But the breeze was gentle. Gentle and in our
faces—which meant that the far side of the bay should have less ice than we
could see from our shore. The ice was still there, but it was spread across the
middle of the bay instead of being packed against either side. We thought
we might just find a way through it.

It was like paddling through a strawberry slushee. Dawn lit the water a
pale sunrise pink. Between the bergs, not a riffle disturbed the glassy reflections. Icebergs rode gently up and down on the swell, some as large as a

table, others barely more than a slurry of ice cubes or a single blade visible above the water.

We worked our way forward, weaving through gaps in the ice. Our boats were tied together again, perched on a long spruce pole attached to the bottom of both packrafts. It was our ramming-bow, shoving smaller bergs aside as we slowly pushed our way through. I watched the icebergs the way people watch clouds—this one a bone, that one a cat's eye, that one the prow of a ship. The mountains and clouds around us cast glowing reflections in the pools between the ice.

"You know, all of those difficulties were just so we could have this crossing," said Hig, clicking away with the camera while I paddled.

"It's beautiful," I agreed.

"It's perfect."

When we finally cleared the ice, we were only a stone's throw from shore. We landed neatly in a tiny notch at the mouth of a river, celebrating with a snack of granola bars before we packed up the rafts and continued on our way.

. . .

After all our trouble getting there, the west side of Icy Bay felt like the end of the world—so remote and difficult to reach, it was hard to imagine anyone being there. Only a scattered handful of souls make this chunk of outer coast their home. But just as we'd seen in Canada, what's too remote for most people doesn't stop logging. From Icy Bay to the Duktoth River, we found one of the largest swaths of clear-cutting we'd hit since southern British Columbia, biting into one of the largest protected areas in the world, the contiguous area of Glacier Bay, Wrangell-St. Elias, and Kluane national parks.

It's a rare patch of forest, in this narrow strip beneath glaciers and peaks. Much of the Lost Coast is too fresh from under the glaciers or too quickly eroding to grow marketable trees. But few trees even in the southernmost reaches of Alaska could compare to west Icy Bay, where a southern exposure and good soil grow a rare wealth of large spruce.

Small waves crashed against the icebergs littering the sandy shore—

nearly lapping the stacks of spruce logs. Rows of logs were lined up in a muddy staging area, waiting for next spring's barge. Two winter watchmen cruised up in a truck, inviting us to stay at their camp for the evening. Refusing a ride, we followed the puddled ruts of their tire tracks as they zoomed ahead.

Five miles down the road, we hit the logging camp. Piles of twisted metal and rubble littered the ground where the logging company had burned several trailers to the ground. After decades of logging in the area, this year had been the last season. The trailer burning was part of shutting the camp down for good.

We spent several hours in conversation with one of the watchmen. He described how much he missed his wife and children back in the Washington town he was from. And he told us about the logging operation.

The largest tree they ever sent out of the Icy Bay camp was thirteen feet in diameter. Many of the smaller trees they never sent out at all. Beyond the camp, we walked past fresh cuts where trees lay piled where they'd fallen—"cull" scrawled on the end of perfectly good timber. Not quite big enough, or straight enough, to be worth shipping to Japan. Lost logs were strewn across Icy Bay's beaches, forming a majority of the wood the reality show participants were using.

"If we did this in Washington," asserted the caretaker, "this wasteful and messy like this, we'd never log a day again in the state."

But western Icy Bay isn't in Washington. It is in one of the more remote corners of a very remote state, on a chunk of land carved out for the Alaska Mental Health Trust Authority. The national parks got the glaciers. The Mental Health Trust got the trees.

Mental Health Trust is charged with using its land to raise money for the state's mental health programs. In this case, as on much of the trust's land, it means selling the trees—clear-cutting not in the patchwork pattern we'd often seen in national forests, but in great swaths across the land. In such a remote location, Mental Health Trust couldn't charge much for its trees. The one who profited most from this enterprise was a Washington-based logging company—Wasser & Winters Co.

The logging crew and all their supplies had been shipped straight from Washington. The raw logs went straight to Japan. And in a place so expensive to ship from, and so far from public view, waste becomes an integral part of the operation.

· · ·

Winter began so gently, we hardly knew it had arrived. A blanket of silvery frost covered the world, sparkling on every blade of beach grass. Ice formed on every pond. The sandy beaches turned hard as concrete.

We woke to mornings lit by moonlight, casting dark shadows on the silvery, frosted beach. As we cooked breakfast, the reds would start creeping into the world to replace the inky black, painting silver-crimson clouds over the ocean and purple skies behind magenta mountains. Then an orange sun boiled up over the surf and slowly crept above the waves. This time of year, the sun traveled sideways all day, hanging low over the ocean and blending imperceptibly between sunrise and sunset.

The morning of December 2 dawned clear and cold. I clutched my coffee mug, huddled by the fire under a dark blue sky as I waited for Hig to finish cooking our spaghetti. Then the stars winked out.

The glimmers of dawn were blotted out by a dark roiling grey. Swirling clouds boiled up to eat the last gaps of slowly brightening blue. Our glittering canopy was replaced by howling snow. It piled and drifted on our gear as we rushed to pack up. The snow buried my pocketknife. Snow fell into the last bites of spaghetti in the pot, quickly chilling them. It whited out all but a hundred feet of beach ahead of us.

It was my birthday. Hig's birthday present to me was to carry my food bag for the day. The world's birthday present was a blizzard. Snow drifted in quickly, covering the frozen beach in a blanket of white. Streaks of blowing snow slashed through the sky in front of craggy black rocks—ending in an impenetrable white wall long before we could even see the ocean. With a tingling excitement that only the change of seasons can bring, I watched the world transformed. I was enthralled.

A yell could barely be heard over the roar, much less a simple comment. With my hood tightly cinched down against the blowing snow, it was an effort even to see Hig walking beside me. We walked silently in a roaring landscape, two feet apart, seeing each other only when we accidentally bumped elbows. I could share neither my enthusiasm, nor my worries.

Were we ready for this? We had warmer clothes. We had a warmer sleeping bag. We had skis.

But all of that gear was sitting in a cardboard box in Valdez, a couple hundred miles beyond where the blizzard raged on Cape Suckling. We'd fallen so far behind our original time estimates that it would be weeks before we could reach our winter gear. On the Lost Coast, our schedule had crumbled into dust. Icy Bay had kept us stuck for a week. And between the short dark days, the obstacles, and the storms, the twenty-mile-per-day estimates we'd made in the comfort of a Seattle apartment seemed laughable.

Winter caught us with only thin nylon rain mitts for gloves. With only a single layer of fleece insulation for our legs beneath the dry suits. With only a one-and-a-half-pound synthetic sleeping bag to keep us warm at night. And we'd been using and wearing all of this gear out for months. We were each on our third pair of shoes and our sixth pair of socks. Both were so torn that it was possible, in one place, to see the bare skin of Hig's foot.

With our modern gear in tatters, we were left with only what we could find around us. We insulated everything with grass—mittens, rafts, our bed. It's an ancient technique, and was surprisingly effective when the grass was dry. The first blizzard was enthralling. But the next storm was far wetter and less welcome, bringing rain along with the snow, soaking everything. With fires increasingly difficult to build from the soggy wood, our wet gear only occasionally got dry. Each night, we slept just a little chillier, snuggling as close as we possibly could in the damp and cold.

· · ·

The mouth of the Copper River Delta is a series of sandbar islands, stretching nearly fifty miles between the river and the surf. Some have patches of spruce forest in the middle. Some appear and disappear with the tide. The world depicted on our map had long since been altered by the shifting of channels, and the land's rise during the 1964 earthquake.

We'd hoped to avoid the delta entirely, taking a route twenty miles farther inland where there was a bridge over the river. But winter had stopped us. Without snowshoes or skis, the foot and a half of fresh wet snow bogged down our progress. Freeze up was an even bigger obstacle. Every creek, stream, and slough was covered with a thin layer of ice—too thin to walk, but too thick to paddle through.

The only way across was to scooch. Kneeling on the seat of the pack-raft, we poled ourselves along with the two halves of the kayak paddle, or leaned out to crawl with arms and elbows on the ice. We were ridiculous, inefficient—scooting across the landscape at a few feet per minute. The packrafts broke through the weak ice in the softer spots, leaving us stranded in tiny pools of water. We exhausted ourselves scooting back up onto intact ice, which often just collapsed again. Even the narrowest creek crossing was a long and difficult ordeal. Twenty miles of postholing and scooching was impossible—we didn't have nearly enough food to fuel such a painstaking way.

Our only way through was to hop between the islands at the mouth of the delta, packrafting from sandbar to sandbar through an eerily empty plain of sand and water—so flat we couldn't tell the river from the land. In the spring, this miles-wide swath of marsh and sandbars is a haven for huge flocks of migratory birds. In summer, salmon teem here on their way to the spawning grounds, and fishermen congregate to catch them. In winter, it's a desolate place—a vast and unnerving obstacle.

. . .

Wind wears on you. At times, it felt as though the world would never stop howling—its shrieks penetrating every last corner of my thoughts. By the third storm in a week, all I wanted was to turn off my ears—to curl up and hide. Rain blew, sheeting across the pools of ice that lay in the low spots between each dune. Even when we were standing still, the wind blew us forward. We slid and spun, unable to stop without falling down or waiting to hit a spot of sand.

We called it Desolate Bar. Wind howled, rain spattered, and nothing but a small patch of dunes rose above the flat sand and the water of the

Copper River Delta. Five miles away, we could see a dim outline of trees on a distant shore. In between, there were only channels, tide flats, and ocean—flat and grey to the edge of the earth. Aside from the beach grass, we were the only living species on our island of sand and ice—miniscule specks in an enormous landscape. It felt as though we were standing in the middle of the ocean. The storm raged around us, churning the delta into a frothing chop we couldn't hope to paddle. We couldn't go anywhere. It was a forsaken world.

The leeward slope of a dune disappeared under the rapid work of our paddle-shovels, creating a blocky sand pit in which to nearly bury our shelter. I gathered armfuls of grass, shoving the makeshift insulation against our thin nylon walls. As we curled up inside, eating a few handfuls from the small bag of peanuts we had remaining, Hig rattled off a list of the storms that had hit us on the Lost Coast. This was number thirteen.

• • •

The next morning, the world was new again. A rose and yellow sunrise lit the fractured layer of clouds and painted the snowy peaks across the river in glowing orange. Their reflections gleamed in the thin sheet of water on the rippled sand flat, along with the bright yellow images of our packrafts. Seagulls sat on ice floes as we wove our way between them, paddling across a wide channel of the Copper River. Harbor seals popped up in the gaps, peering at us with permanently curious expressions.

It was nearly six months from the start of our journey. And so far, the Lost Coast was my favorite place in over 2,000 miles of country. As we conceived of it, much of the Lost Coast was the very definition of wilderness. A place that didn't notice or care whether we were there or not. A place not set up for humans, and outside of human rules.

There's something awesome about setting yourself under nature's rules—something that transcends comfort. The intensity of the Lost Coast was like nothing we'd ever experienced. And when it was gorgeous, it was the most gorgeous place on earth.

. . .

From the Copper River Delta, we walked thirty-five miles into Cordova in a single day. With seven miles of wading through slush, and twenty-eight miles of trudging on a mostly empty road, the pull of food and warmth and shelter spurred us on for our longest walking day of the trip. Sometime near midnight, a car pulled over as we slowly trudged to town, stopping to chat, and to offer us their congratulations on our accomplishment.

Cordova was the first place we really began to hear congratulations. It was the first time people spent as much time being impressed by what we'd already done as they spent being amazed, skeptical, or incredulous of what we were planning. We needed to hear it. But even though we'd just finished the Lost Coast, we were only a little over halfway to Unimak Island. And there was plenty of winter left to come.

10. HEART OF WINTER

Erin: "Ski bushwhacking in the winter
is like summer with about eighteen extra
helpings of pain."

WE GREETED WINTER SOLSTICE with a bonfire. On Prince William Sound, beyond the surf of the Lost Coast, small waves lapped on our gravel beach. Delicate cascades of icicles spilled over boulders and cliffs, where forests once again reached nearly to the water's edge. Cooking finished, we sat for hours, just watching the dance of the flames. Finally, we let the last coals die and stirred the gravel until it was evenly warm, heating the ground beneath our bed.

The bear-proof bags we carried to store our food were filled with warm gravel—transformed into heated pillows for our heads and feet. Our food lay scattered in dry bags around us.

For months already, we'd been sleeping nearly on top of our food—not a recommended practice in bear country. During the long summer days, we had cooked our dinners in the middle of the day, far from where we slept. But on rainy fall nights, we often cooked under the flap of the tent. And the more we traveled in bear country, the more we became convinced that in these rarely traveled areas, avoiding bears at night had little to do with food and more to do with a careful choice of campsite. We simply slept where they would be unlikely to travel. Bears not accustomed to campers don't seek them out.

Skiing through beetle-killed black spruce in Copper Basin

But the bears were asleep now. And we continued into winter.

At Cordova we had turned away from the open Pacific Ocean, and for the last several days we'd been packrafting the protected waters of Prince William Sound. When we reached Valdez, we planned to leave the coast entirely to follow the inland side of the Chugach Mountains—through the frigid interior climate of Copper River Basin.

In our Valdez host's basement, we opened the Christmas presents we had mailed to ourselves, eagerly tearing apart boxes containing our thick down quilt, warm mittens, and secondhand skis. I envisioned skis swishing across sunlit fields of snow, mountain peaks lit rosy pink in sunset, blazing fires under starry skies. I pictured myself flying across a winter wonderland, the shiny blue skis strapped to my feet. The half-frozen morass of the Copper River Delta was fading into memory. And the winter seemed full of a sparkling promise.

· · ·

Five days beyond Valdez, and twenty feet ahead of me on a steep and lumpy hillside, Hig was leaning back with his right ski high in the air, trying to fit it between the twisted branches of a snowy alder. I watched him struggle, standing thigh-deep in powder snow with my skis in my hand, debating whether to put them back on. My ski tips knocked against a branch, sending a shower of snow down my collar. The air was still, cold, and unnervingly quiet. Each snowflake settled just where it fell, coating even the most delicate twigs in puffs of white. The snow was dry and powdery—nearly weightless. We sunk nearly as much with our skis as we sunk without them.

Which was the worst of the evils—carrying the skis as an awkward bundle while sinking waist-deep into the fluffy snow, or trying to maneuver my six-foot-long feet through six-inch-wide spaces between the branches?

It had been hours since we had left the road near Thompson Pass, where the highway and oil pipeline from Valdez cut through the Chugach Mountains. On the map, the distance between highway and alpine terrain had seemed almost imperceptibly small. But we were barely making headway. And there was no winter wonderland in sight.

The following afternoon found us still firmly stuck in that same "imperceptibly small" chunk of space. In fact, it had only gotten worse. We crashed through tangles of brush and waded through chest-deep snow, but this time on slopes that were even steeper, weaving around a scattering of rocky cliffs. We didn't have skins for our skis. But mired in a thicket in sinky snow, it hardly even mattered.

We took the skis off, put them on, took them off, put them on... I couldn't decide which was worse. Frustrated, I ditched my skis, my pack, and my ski poles—charging up the slope with an aggravated roar. Some of my frustration vented, I quickly realized that ditching the stuff had helped. We made our way through the worst spots with a gear-carrying bucket brigade: One person charged ahead while the second person stomped up and down the slope behind them, ferrying the skis and all of the gear— sometimes four trips for each tiny piece of terrain. It took us almost a day to go three quarters of a mile. Finally, just in time for sunset, we popped out above the tree line, flying quickly across wind-packed snow—trying not to think about how we had to descend again the next day.

• • •

Beyond that bushwhack, we did everything we could to keep our skis to the brush-free expanses of icy lakes or along the winding corridors of small creeks. Our route meandered with the waterways, quickly ballooning into something far longer than we'd originally planned.

This early in the winter, the ice on the creeks was thin. Ice shelves dropped off into open pools of dark blue where frost crystals grew long and delicate along the edge. Twice I had plunged my feet through too-thin ice, filling my ski boots with water that quickly began to freeze in the below-zero air. I filled them with snow to dry them as much as I could, and then spent the rest of the day skiing in socks with frozen edges, forced to sleep in them to dry them out.

Sometimes we followed a creek that was still entirely open—forcing us into the tangle of brush along the side. Even where the ice was solid, it was covered with a foot or two of loose and fluffy snow too light to hold our skis. We shuffled through it, trading off which of us broke trail, and which of us pulled our gear in the packrafts behind. Our progress was slow and painstaking. Combined with the short winter days, the difficulties of Copper River Basin had shrunk our daily mileage to the smallest it had been on the entire trip—less than nine miles in each hard day of travel. Like many times before, we were running low on food. And while our short days burned fewer calories than we'd been used to, the frigid nights burned more.

Until we lost our cheap thermometer somewhere in a snowy forest, it had been reading average temperatures below zero degrees Fahrenheit. Twice it dipped to minus seventeen degrees, probably going beyond the accurate range of a thermometer that registered temperatures only to minus twenty degrees Fahrenheit. When we returned to civilization, we heard that it had actually dropped as low as minus thirty.

We looked pregnant. We looked like boxy kangaroos. Food, water, cameras—everything that wouldn't stand freezing—was stuffed against our bellies, inside several layers of coats. Potato chips were one of the only things we could eat straight from our packs. Nearly everything else, from bags of "Buttery Goodness" to blocks of cheese, to chocolate and granola bars, had to be carried next to our skin for half the day before it warmed enough to be edible. Even one layer out, our water bottles would freeze.

Luckily, acclimation happens surprisingly quickly. On the Lost Coast and in Prince William Sound, we probably hadn't seen weather colder than fifteen degrees. But by a week into our traverse of Copper River Basin, zero felt normal. Ten was incredibly warm. But when the temperature dropped toward minus twenty, it seemed to take half an hour of skiing just to warm our feet and fingers. During the day, we rarely stopped moving.

To sleep, we carried a homemade down quilt, tucked inside the synthetic half-bag (insulation on top, but not on the bottom) we'd carried the whole way. We slept on a pair of three-quarter-length inflatable sleeping pads, on top of a larger sheet of thin white foam. At just under five-and-a-half pounds for the pair of us, this set up could keep us warm even in minus twenty, as long as we were wearing all our insulation—with only our noses exposed to the frigid air. Sharing body heat helped tremendously. But the water that evaporated from our bodies froze before it escaped the bag. Each night, a little more ice accumulated in the insulation.

· · ·

"Eww! I think I smell another one!" I yelled across the crackle of our bonfire. "Over there, I think."

Hig approached the offending patch of snow with a pair of sticks, gingerly picking up last summer's rotten salmon and flinging it beyond the radius of our fire. As our fire burned down through the snow on the banks of the Klutina River, the previously hard-frozen fish beneath it thawed, wafting their odors across our camp. But even in winter, these fish were a critical piece of the food chain. Tracks of eagles and coyotes laced the banks, where they had scraped holes to unearth the salmon from the snow. Brown crumbs of long-rotten fish were strewn around them.

Flames roared four feet into the air, sending a geyser of sparks above our heads. I rearranged our synthetic bag where it hung over a propped-up log, noting a new burn hole before turning another side to the heat—hoping to thaw the frost clumps that had accumulated in the insulation. In the bitter cold, our life revolved around the three pillars of warmth: fires, skiing, and the sleeping bag. When we weren't skiing to keep warm, or huddled deep within our layers of insulation, we built fires. Enormous fires—keeping us going through cooking and camp tasks—brightening a few of the many hours of winter dark. We reveled in the cone of warmth, throwing on larger and larger logs.

Firewood was rarely more than an arm's length away. Most of the spruce trees in the valleys we'd been skiing were dead—cambium eaten away by the spruce bark beetle. Skinny poles of beetle-killed spruce filled the forest, leaning at crazy angles, littering the floor with sharp dead logs. Starting a fire was as easy as breaking off the tops of a few small dead trees and holding a match beneath them.

In Southcentral Alaska, the spruce bark beetle has always waged a low-level war with the trees. Most of the time, the beetles ate only downed trees. Every fifty years or so, they would break out, killing patches of live forest. The bigger and older spruce were particularly vulnerable. For a long time, this was the pattern. Between 1920 and 1990, the beetle killed two-and-a-half million acres of spruce—36,000 acres per year.

But in the 1990s, the beetles went into overdrive. Some researchers blame climate change. It takes cool wet summers—historically common in this part of Alaska—to knock the beetles down. A series of unbroken warm summers let the beetle population explode, sometimes going through an entire reproductive cycle in half the usual time, eating not just the mature trees, but sometimes every tree standing.

As we traveled north, the rainforest's tree species had disappeared one by one. Somewhere in southern British Columbia, we'd lost the Douglas firs, the madronas, and the bigleaf maples. In northern British Columbia, the silver fir and yew had vanished. In Southeast Alaska, the red cedars and red alders disappeared. Then the pines and the yellow cedars. And since we'd left Prince William Sound at Valdez, we hadn't seen a single hemlock. This far north, spruce are no longer just one little piece of a diverse forest. Spruce is pretty much all that can grow.

In the 1990s, four million acres of spruce trees were infested and killed in just ten years—wiping out up to 80 percent of the trees in the hardest-hit areas. At 400,000 acres per year, the epidemic killed at eleven times the beetle's usual rate—ending only when the bugs ran out of trees to eat.

• • •

Before we could see the ribbon of pavement, before we could even hear the cars, we could smell it. Hanging in the cold still air, the scent of grime, rubber, and exhaust was unmistakable. The Glenn Highway.

At that moment, we welcomed it. Along our traverse through Copper River Basin, we'd found a shut-down lodge where we had managed to thoroughly dry our icy sleeping bag and grab a little extra food. But that had been days ago. Hungry and tired, we intersected the highway near Eureka. A generous family provided us with food before we even hit the first highway roadhouse. But it wouldn't be long before we were desperately wishing for a better way.

Copper River Basin is a pool of frigid air—a high pressure zone trapped in a low spot between four mountain ranges: the Wrangells, the Chugach, the Talkeetnas, and the Alaska Range. Within the basin, the air is calm. But in the big river valleys that slice through the mountains, wind howls—the pressure differential sending cold air pouring from Copper River Basin into the coastal areas around it. We'd passed through this wind twice before; at the Copper River Delta, and again on the Lowe River as it cut through the mountains near Valdez.

Now that same wind screamed through the narrow corridor between the Chugach and Talkeetna Mountains—the corridor that was the only way to Anchorage. The Glenn Highway shares this narrow notch with the Matanuska River. With no room for any other path, we bounced back and forth between them.

• • •

We skied along the river. Snow blowing up from the ground blended with the snow blowing down from the sky, until we were skiing through a whirling white haze. The thin cover of snow we'd been skiing on gave way to patches of bare gravel, and then to glare ice. In the heart of a deep and narrow gorge, the South Fork Matanuska River was a sheet of slippery turquoise.

The packrafts we'd been pulling as gear sleds took off in a gust, strewing our food bags and dry bags across the ice. We tried to dig the metal edges of our skis into the ice, to little avail. With our bodies as sails, the wind sent us hurtling downstream on a ride that was nearly uncontrollable. To stop, I had to fall.

I fell. I took off my skis, unsure whether the ice beneath me would hold me without them. In the end, we crawled on hands and knees across the icy channels until we were past the worst of the gorge. It might have only been a hundred yards. But it was enough. We returned to the highway.

• • •

We walked along the highway. Both of my fancy ski boots were cracked wide open, straight across the width of the toe box. Hig's were the same. I fruitlessly dug a few snowballs out with the thumb of my mitten, the snow grimy brown with the dirt and dust of traffic. I reached under my shoulder straps, trying to arrange the weight of my pack a little more comfortably. The six awkward pounds of my skis made a heavy tower above my head.

We scrunched farther toward the edge of the road as a car hurtled by, headlights blazing. I watched it go, picturing a climate-controlled bubble of warmth and music. For that driver, the one hundred road miles between us and our next stop in Palmer was only a trivial couple hours of travel. Our feet grew sore. The mileage markers were an ever-crueler reminder of how far we had to go. We returned to the river.

• • •

We grew grumpier and grumpier. Perhaps it was the darkness. In the past fifteen days, we'd seen bright sun for perhaps fifteen minutes. In the depths of January, the sun remained firmly below and behind the Chugach Mountains, rarely rising to a place where we could see it. And even when it appeared in the sky, ice fog left it a pale weak version of itself. Generally easily compatible, Hig and I got into more and more arguments as we traveled toward Anchorage. We were trapped between two bad options.

Four times we left the highway for the river. Each time, Hig argued for giving the river another chance, pleading that it was *so much more interesting than the terrible road*. And each time, we ran into a nearly impossible morass. A river scoured naked by the wind—howling along over frozen cobbles, glare ice, overflow, and chasms dropping down to open water. At times, we skied along smooth sheets of wind-packed snow between scenic bluffs and grazing moose, but that wasn't often. And those good sections couldn't compensate for the mess that was the rest of the river. And it was all Hig's fault.

Four times we left the river for the road. Each time, I argued for just heading out to the road, pleading that it was the only practical way and that we needed to *just get this bit over with and be done with it*. And each time, our feet grew sore in clomping ski boots. We trudged through the dirty snow kicked up by the rumbling snowplows, squeezing onto the shoulder as cars screamed past, each one deafening us and leaving us with a lingering stench of exhaust. The awful monotony was broken only by the occasional greasy spoon selling hamburgers and fries. We hated it more than we'd hated any part of any trip we'd ever done. And it was all my fault.

• • •

For the last miles into Anchorage, a trail follows the highway, ten feet from the roaring column of traffic. Gritty snow thrown by the snowplow piled on our path. A continual stream of headlights flashed past, casting our long shadows over the snow. There was rarely even a tree between us and the road, allowing us to use the highway signs to count down the miles as we traveled.

We turned onto Muldoon Road, suddenly trading the whizzing headlights for street lamps and glowing neon. We'd been pulling one of the packrafts as a sled along the trail. Now on the city sidewalks, we realized that the valve was encrusted with ice and completely impossible to unscrew and deflate. So we threw the skis on the boat, tugging it along the sidewalk, trying to keep it from skittering into traffic. We wore strange-looking dry suits and ratty fur-ruff hoods pulled over our heads.

A couple of teenagers in the parking lot yelled to us derisively: "Where are you going? Nome?"

I smiled. Unimak Island was actually quite a bit farther than Nome, but those kids were more right than they could have known.

I could care less what anyone thought of me. We trailed the packraft behind us as we walked past video stores and pizza joints, loading it with bulging bags of groceries. Ice cream. Fresh vegetables. Each neon sign shone like a welcome beacon. We were planning to spend two weeks in Anchorage—a well-earned vacation.

11. ESCAPING THE ROAD

*Erin: "You know, that's probably the
first pizza delivery ever to Lake Clark Pass."*

SOMETIMES PEOPLE ALONG the way would ask how the journey had
changed us. At the beginning, I didn't think it would. We weren't out to
experience epiphanies of self-discovery—we wanted to discover something
about the world.

But slowly and subtly, the world changed around us, and we changed
with it. Physically, we got in better and better shape. We learned to adapt to
the seasons as they came—to the horseflies and heat of the B.C. coast, the
rain of Southeast Alaska, the winds of the Lost Coast, and the bitter cold of
Copper Basin. But the biggest changes came in perception.

I had never spent so much time in my life just noticing things: the
intense smell of a broken spruce branch in cold still air, the tracks of a tiny
pine siskin, the sliding trail of a river otter, the sound of cracking ice. Much
of the world was snow. So we noticed the heavy wetness of warm snow,
the weightless fluff of cold snow, the elaborate crystals built by the frost, its
swish or squeak or crunch beneath our feet. Nothing was bright or loud.
Nothing screamed for our attention. There were only the details. And the
details mattered—only subtle differences in snow texture distinguishing a
safe place to ski from a spot of too-thin ice. There were no written signs
to explain what we saw. We discovered the world by watching, listening,
and smelling. Our senses were heightened, and even in Anchorage, I found

Hig is silhouetted against the setting sun on a snow-covered ridge above Cook Inlet.

myself constantly examining the world for clues: staring at dishes and book-cases the way I'd peer at tracks in the snow, asking them questions I might have otherwise asked our hosts.

· · ·

We spent two weeks in Anchorage—the longest we'd stopped anywhere along our journey. Despite the minus twenty-degree temperatures, we zipped around the city on studded-tire bicycles we'd borrowed from a friend, sticking to our "No Motorized Transport" rule through the longest cold snap Anchorage had seen in years.

Both of our mothers and Hig's father flew to Anchorage to see us. We visited with old friends and met several new ones. We were interviewed by reporters from newspapers and radio. We presented a slideshow to a crowded auditorium, telling everyone about all that we'd done so far.

Hig spent hours seated at a borrowed sewing machine, reconstruct-ing our grubby and torn gear with swatches of bright new fabric. What we couldn't repair, we replaced. Our sponsors happily sent us new versions of their gear (for us to destroy). We were the grateful recipients of a third set of dry suits, new spray decks, our third pyramid shelter, and after our frigid days in Copper Basin, yet another layer of puffy synthetic coats and pants.

Our time in Anchorage wasn't really a vacation, but a regrouping. We had planned as much of the trip as possible before we left Seattle. But now, from food, to gear repairs, to route details, to the logistics of meeting up with people in towns, it seemed that we prepared for each leg on the fly, in a whirlwind of activity at each of our resupply points. Anchorage was our chance to pore over and print out new maps, to bike to the outdoor store for new ski boots and the other odds and ends we still needed. To plan. Our two weeks of relaxing quickly turned into two weeks of meetings and errands and frenzied activity—spending money left and right and biking grimy roads alongside hurtling, oblivious cars. We were ready to re-exit civilization.

· · ·

Even in my dreams, ice swirled. It flowed back and forth with the tides—a rushing, shearing mass of grey and white. Ice floes formed a dancing maze—opening filigrees of dark leads between them, and then smashing together in a solid block of slush, edges crumbling as they collided. The shadows of buildings flashed on and off against the whirls of white. Tugboats stood in silhouette, pushing through water that was barely even liquid. The world was full of motion but devoid of any obvious life—a rushing current of ice. The skyscrapers of downtown Anchorage stood watch over the most desolate, unnerving, and wild place we'd seen since the Copper River Delta: Knik Arm.

We were trying to escape the road. Our destination lay on the other side of Cook Inlet—two miles west of Anchorage—just across the narrow point of Knik Arm. Skiing around the channel would take us at least four days and bring us back along roads and roaring highway-parallel trails that we were willing to do almost anything to avoid. Paddling across would take only two hours in open water. If open water existed.

A small crowd of packrafters—friends from Anchorage—had joined us for an attempted crossing. Five of us stood on an ice pan a dozen feet wide as the world spun in confusing procession, giving us first a view of giant container stacks at the Anchorage port, then golden beams of sunset glinting off a vast sweep of jumbled ice and the unattainable hills beyond.

Our paddles chopped into a thick slush of skim ice. We struggled through narrow leads, grunting and shoving as the world solidified around us. Walls of ice formed suddenly between the rafts. Twenty feet apart might as well have been a mile. The tide swept the world sideways. Fifty feet from shore, we worked hard to regain it, measuring our progress in spinning inches. It seemed we'd invited our friends to join a foolish dream.

We twisted our way back through the bergs, back to the safety of the city shore. Dark fell over the Arm as we shared beers in the Snow Goose Bar, our friends remarking how odd it was to be in a bar wearing dry suits, while Hig and I wore ours as though they were the only clothes we owned. We speculated. Would a different tide or launch spot have let us through the maze? Was crossing Knik Arm even possible?

Each time an errand brought us downtown, we'd stop and stare across the icy water—standing on a snowy bench while skiers and dog-walkers cruised past on the trail behind us. It was a "look but don't touch" wilderness. The tidal range in Knik Arm is over thirty feet. In the narrow neck between Anchorage and Point MacKenzie, the currents run fast and wild. In the summer, sinking mudflats provide a barrier between land and water. In winter, ice swirls, binding and crunching until it's difficult to tell if there is any water at all. As far as we knew, no one had ever paddled a small craft across Knik Arm in the winter.

After our aborted effort with our friends, we tried alone. On our next attempt, we barely escaped spending the night in the shifting currents and ice of upper Cook Inlet. Halfway across, we were nearly frozen in.

We raced back to Anchorage through the narrow leads between ice floes as each dark ribbon slammed shut behind us, always one step ahead of impenetrable floating slush—an action movie escape. Our retreat was closing fast, just behind us, but each time we managed to squeak through.

Day after day, we returned to Knik Arm, staring across the ice-choked water, willing an open path that never came. Each time I looked out at that jumble of ice, it seemed more malevolent than the day before—rapidly turning from an obstacle to an enemy.

. . .

"Sometimes, the hardest lesson to learn is when to turn around." I typed the line into my blog post in an Eagle River motel, two days after that second crossing attempt, and one day after giving up on Knik Arm.

When we had drawn the original line—the plan dreamed up in Seattle—crossing Knik Arm had seemed the most sensible way to go. Even if it was a difficult crossing, it was only two miles, and it would take us straight to where we needed to go.

By the time we reached Anchorage, Knik Arm was the salvation that would let us escape the highway. At that point, I'd have done anything to avoid the several days of roadside drudgery it would take to ski around.

But after two weeks in Anchorage, Knik Arm had become a mission. After covering more than 2,500 miles, including packrafting across Portland Canal and through the ice-choked waters of the Hubbard Gap, Icy Bay, and the Copper River Delta, I was reluctant to believe that two miles of water could be impossible.

We persuaded friends to set up time-lapse cameras trained on the icy channel. We spent hours poring over the resulting videos, analyzing how the ice responded to the swirling tides. We scouted the crossing more times than I could count, dragging our packrafts out to the coastal trail or simply staring across the gap. We discussed every variable—every shift in the temperature, wind, and tide. We waffled back and forth for days, debating whether to give up, or to wait just one more day. I think we spent more time preparing for these two miles than we had spent preparing for the other 2,500 miles of the trip so far. But it didn't matter. The Arm refused to budge into a resolvable puzzle.

Knik Arm won. We skied around it.

• • •

On the far side of Knik Arm, after our days-long detour, we looked southwest along a line of snowy volcanoes rising above the coastal marshes of Cook Inlet. We had passed the northernmost point of our journey. We had left the road net behind. And that line of volcanoes would lead us along the Alaska Peninsula and eventually to the Aleutian Islands.

In the inlet, flaming skeletons of distant drill rigs stood on the horizon—spooky silhouettes against a sickly yellow sunset. Snow-machine tracks ran over the buried natural gas pipeline, leaving an icy corridor for us to ski. We counted down the miles to the Beluga Power Plant: 19, 17, 15,...7, 5, 3, 1....

It loomed over us in the dark—a monstrous contraption of concrete and pipes, spookily lit by industrial yellow-orange lamps. We had to shout to hear each other over the constant screeching metallic howl. The largest power plant in Alaska, the Beluga natural gas plant powers a good chunk of the state's "rail belt" power grid, with Anchorage at its heart. But gas isn't the only fossil carbon beneath the hills of Beluga.

Some hope Alaska will become the "Saudi Arabia of coal." Others fear it. An eighth of the world's coal reserves lie beneath the Alaskan wilderness—half of the coal in the United States. The largest deposits lie in the northwest Arctic. Most of the rest can be found in the Cook Inlet basin. And almost all of it is still in the ground.

But if PacRim Coal, LP, has its way, that coal won't stay in the ground. Ten miles from Beluga, we switchbacked on our skinless skis to the top of a small and rounded hill, covered with twisted birch. All around us similar hills popped up from a rumpled landscape of frozen wetlands, meadows, and ponds. It could all become a strip mine.

The proposed Chuitna Coal Mine would obliterate eight square miles of landscape. Everything we could see would be bulldozed, mined, and drained, including eleven miles of salmon-spawning streams. If it goes through, it will be the first time a large mine in Alaska is allowed to mine right through salmon-bearing waters. Giant pumps would dewater the ground, dumping seven million gallons of mine runoff per day into the Chuitna River. From the mine to the inlet, crushed coal would rattle for miles down a half-open conveyor belt, potentially scattering coal dust across the land. Twelve million tons of coal per year.

From the residents of Beluga, we heard a litany of fears and concerns about the project's potential consequences—for the salmon they caught in the Chuitna River and Cook Inlet beyond, for the endangered beluga whales of the inlet, for their businesses, their food, and their health. Listening to them, I also wondered about consequences further afield. Alaska doesn't burn much coal now, and exports the excess from the state's only coal mine as far away as Chile. What happens when the coal is burned? Carbon dioxide will rise into the atmosphere, warming our world, melting the glaciers of the Lost Coast, perhaps hastening the decline of the toads in Southeast Alaska, and helping the spruce bark beetle in its battle with the trees.

When we were in Beluga, in early 2008, PacRim Coal was working on its final permit applications, which would set off the official review process. Only a few small clues hinted at this land's potential future: orange survey stakes, a weather station, the landing tracks of a helicopter surrounded by snowshoe prints from biologists checking a fish-trap, stray bits of bright pink flagging tape. It was hard to imagine what it might become.

We climbed a bluff above the Chuitna River, feeling the warmth of the sun on our backs, looking out over the crinkled folds of the river gorge and the craggy mass of Mount Spurr rising behind it. The brown dot of a moose crossed the river below us. Long shadows of scraggly spruce bent over the rounded contours of snow-filled gullies. Our skis swished through a thin layer of powder on top of a hard crust of gleaming icy snow. It was the first truly beautiful skiing we'd had all winter.

Leaving Chuitna behind, we headed over the mountains—toward Lake Iliamna and another potential mine.

· · ·

The first time we saw the plane, I fell. It buzzed past with a deafening roar that made it sound as though it was about to land right on top of me. I swiveled to look, and my skis ricocheted off a bump on the slick ice of Big River, dropping me to the ground and smashing my knee into the ice. Propped on one elbow, I looked up, watching the bottom side of a little beige 206 as it zoomed up Lake Clark Pass. I waved, embarrassed, and the plane waggled its wings to wave back.

On our maps, Lake Clark Pass is covered by a pair of glaciers spilling across the valley. But they've retreated since the maps were drawn, hanging in turquoise jumbles on the steep valley walls. No one walks (or skis) through this narrow notch between forbidding mountains.

But every little plane is funneled through. The pass is the primary air traffic corridor between Anchorage and the small villages on Lake Clark and Lake Iliamna. As we skied between the mountains lining the Big River and Tlikakila valleys, we were the one thing out of place in the flyway. Each day the planes buzzed low over our heads, waving to the only spots of color in their otherwise unchanging route.

A few days later, we waved at the beige plane again, recognizing it easily from its twice-daily passes overhead. But after it had buzzed us three times in ten minutes, we were totally confused. The roar of the prop thundered over us a fourth time. As we watched the plane recede, a white plastic bag appeared in the sky, trailing yellow streamers as it fluttered to the ground.

It was a pizza. It was a pizza from the Moose's Tooth—which makes some of the best pizza in Anchorage. It was a pizza loaded with sausage and peppers and onions and tomatoes and a whole pile of other goodies we didn't bother to list before devouring it. It was a pizza with a friendly note from the pilot who'd dropped it, inviting us to stop by when we got to Port Alsworth. It wasn't exactly hot, but in the ten-degree weather, it was easily the warmest food we had.

"You know," I said as I grabbed another piece, "that's probably the first pizza delivery ever to Lake Clark Pass."

• • •

My skis swished and swooshed on the far side of Lake Clark Pass, gliding through a thin layer of soft powder over a hard wind-packed base, following the gentle descent of the Tlikakila River. I felt as though I was flying. The sun came out, lighting the peaks around us, warming the left sides of our bodies. Windblown river otter tracks laced the ground. We photographed everything.

It was the first of March. If we had been correct in our initial calculations, we would have been nearly at the Aleutians by now. But if we'd been here much earlier, the sun would never have touched down into the depths of the Tlikakila Valley. Our sparkling winter visions were finally coming true. And as we approached nine months of travel, I felt a new inspiration for the thousand miles still remaining.

12. PEBBLE

Hig: "To a geologist, forever doesn't even make sense!"

THE TLIKAKILA RIVER dropped us into lake country, in the midst of a howling rainstorm. Ever since we'd left the landlocked Copper Basin, we'd left the extreme cold behind—trading it back for the wind. Wind screamed across the melted sheen of water on the frozen surface of Little Lake Clark, sending us flying across the ice. Water sprayed up from the tips of my skis as though I were a hydroplaning boat. I dug my ski poles into the ice—ineffective brakes—sending shavings skittering along the slick wet surface. Cliffs and trees on the shore zipped past at a speed I hadn't experienced since giving up motorized transport.

From Little Lake Clark, we would join Lake Clark, then Sixmile Lake, and eventually the eighty-mile-long expanse of Lake Iliamna. We were entering a rolling landscape of glacier-carved lakes. Beneath our feet, baby sockeye salmon waited for the thaw, preparing for their journey to the sea. In the sea, silvery giants fattened up for next summer's journey back to the lakes where they'd been born. We had crossed the divide from the Pacific Ocean, and the lakes we now skied on drain into Bristol Bay, part of the Bering Sea. Tens of millions of salmon return to this region each year, reaching these lakes through a series of remote and wild rivers. As they arrive, they feed everything from trees to bears to people, supporting the world's largest commercial sockeye fishery.

At a meeting in Nondalton village, elders highlight subsistence use areas on a map of the Pebble prospect area.

We'd left the Chuitna Coal Mine proposal behind in the hills near Beluga, but we were closing in on another potential mine—Pebble. Where PacRim Coal envisioned a wealth of coal, Pebble Limited Partnership was seeking an even greater wealth of copper and gold.

Sometime in this region's distant past, vast underground seas of magma-heated water flowed up through fractured rock, precipitating metals in cracks and pockets beneath the surface. The vast reserves of copper and gold here don't show up as even a fleck or a sparkle in the ordinary grey rocks. But it's enough for the mining company, with their chemical analysis, to see billions of dollars.

If Pebble Mine is built, it will be one of the most massive works of man. Great earthen walls would reach 750 feet above a remote valley floor between Lake Clark and Lake Iliamna, damming off a storage area for the mine's toxic tailings. The tailings lake would cover more than eight square miles, with dams larger than the Three Gorges Dam in China. The open pit would reach down farther into the valley floor than the 3,000-foot mountains that rise above it—creating one of the largest open pit mines on the continent. Tunnels would snake out from the bottom of the pit, seeking out deeper ore, collapsing and consuming the mountains above them.

Two knee-deep creeks run through this remote valley of willow and tundra. Hundreds of miles away, these creeks empty into Bristol Bay as two great rivers, the Nushagak and the Kvichak. The Pebble prospect sits in a wetland, on a drainage divide, between two of the most productive salmon rivers in the world.

Until a few years ago, few outsiders had ever visited the Pebble valley. Outside the mining prospect, it never even had a name. But now it was becoming famous.

Even in development-friendly Alaska, this proposal has set off a firestorm of controversy. Some hope to make money: The mining company hopes for profits, state and local governments hope for taxes, and locals hope for jobs. Some fear destruction: Environmental groups fear destruction of the wilderness, commercial fishermen and tourism operators fear destruction of their livelihoods, and locals fear destruction of the salmon and wildlife that are their subsistence.

This was the third time in four years we'd visited the area, plunging ourselves into the thick of the controversy. We'd researched the issue, tramped the 450 miles of downstream rivers with camera in hand, and worked to spread our information however we could. So when we skied into Nondalton village, we were returning to familiar ground.

• • •

A cluster of low, colorful buildings emerged from the bare birch and shaggy spruce on the shores of Sixmile Lake. The small forms of people appeared on the edge of the ice, approaching to greet us.

"Come in! There's moose stew and all kinds of food."

We were led into a packed community center, where we lined up for styrofoam bowls of moose stew and paper plates packed with all kinds of treats, greeting old acquaintances. Pictures I'd taken a couple years earlier covered a poster near the door. We dumped our snowy backpacks in a corner, and sat down for a meeting on the proposed Pebble Mine.

Anti-mine symbols graced buttons and baseball caps around the room—a neat red slash through the words "Pebble Mine." "No Pebble Mine" posters covered the walls, the professional work of an Anchorage environmental group intermingled with the colorful hand-drawn efforts of local children. Nunamta Aulukestai, a multi-village organization firmly against the mining proposal, had invited a panel of scientists to talk about the potential impacts of a mine. They had also invited one of the state officials involved in permitting.

The scientists stood up to talk about the hydrology of the proposed mine site, the mine's potential effects on the area's salmon, and the problematic track records of other U.S. mines. Their concerns centered around one big issue—acid mine drainage. The gold and copper under Pebble valley isn't found in glistening nuggets or shimmering veins. Like a lot of modern mining prospects, it comes bound up with sulfur, stirred into a great mix of metal sulfides. Buried in the earth, sulfides are safe. But when they're dug up, ground up, and exposed to air and water, they start to react. Sulfides turn to sulfuric acid, which leaches into streams and ground water, carrying toxic heavy metals along with it, killing fish and life within its path.

When it was his turn to speak, Tom Crafford, the Large Mine Coordinator from the Alaska Department of Natural Resources, flashed slide after slide of flow charts and long lists of tiny text, trying to explain the permitting process. All I retained from the first part of his talk was that mine permitting is complicated—involving many different agencies and many different steps. But the question and answer session at the end of his presentation turned to a different issue—cleanup. What would happen if the mining company went bankrupt? How much money would they have to put up to protect against any future disasters? Over the long term, what would keep those acid-generating mine tailings from leaching into the water? What would keep the rivers safe?

Crafford explained the setup at Red Dog Mine, a zinc mine in northern Alaska, where a water-treatment plant sits at the outlet of the tailings storage lake, perpetually deacidifying and detoxifying the water before it is released, making it safe for downstream life. When the mine closes, the treatment plant will still be there, treating the water in perpetuity. Other maintenance will need to be performed perpetually as well, keeping the toxic tailings stored in a dammed-off lake, forever sequestered away from water and air.

One of the invited experts spoke up—saying that he didn't think it was wise to permit any mine that required perpetual water treatment. Crafford didn't answer whether or not the state would permit a mine like that again. And no one knows yet whether Pebble would require such a treatment plant. But it would definitely require dams and maintenance—in perpetuity.

Hig broke in with a question of his own, "What exactly do you mean by 'in perpetuity?'"

"Forever," Crafford responded.

"Actually forever?"

"Yes."

"When the United States no longer exists, when glaciers roll over the landscape in another ten thousand years, some guy is going to be out there with a bulldozer maintaining the dams around the tailings storage lake? To a geologist, forever doesn't even make sense!"

I doubt anyone else in the room really cared about the theoretical people of ten thousand years from now, but Hig had a point. Forever was impossible. Whether it happened in one year, ten years, a hundred years, or a thousand, those tailings would eventually pollute the downstream watersheds. Failure was a given. We were just taking bets on when it might happen, and how rapid a failure it might be.

· · ·

After one more night in Nondalton, we left for the Pebble prospect. Pebble valley lies sixteen miles outside the village, a glacier-carved trough surrounded by low, rounded mountains. When I'd seen it in the summer, hundreds of shallow lakes and ponds sparkled in the wet tundra that blankets the valley floor. When I'd seen it in fall, berries speckled the tundra with a rainbow of sweet-tasting gems. Now in March, the landscape was brushed smooth with a coat of white, crisscrossed by the tracks of foxes and porcupines. On the hills above the valley, golden streams of snow blew across the ground, lit by a hazy sunset. Winter-coated ptarmigan erupted from their snowy beds, white balls of feathers nearly invisible against their white surroundings.

We approached the prospect from the peak of Groundhog Mountain, where we hoped we might look out over the valley. But a puffy white flood filled the world around us. Only the tops of distant peaks poked out above the cottony thick layer of clouds.

All we could see was a gorgeous moment: distant snowy volcanoes, the sea of clouds, sun sparkling on feathers of frost, and ice crystal rainbows. But as we snacked on our bag of Grape Nuts, most of what we could hear was a fleet of invisible helicopters in the valley below—the thrumming roar of industry. We skied down the hill, practicing our turns, swishing back and forth on the gentle slope, dropping through the whiteout—on our way to a whole different world.

A ribbon of dark bare willows snaked through the smooth white landscape, marking the banks of Upper Talarik Creek as it flowed through the Pebble valley. The tops of brush and stubby trees poked through the snow, along with the towers of the drill rigs exploring the mining prospect. Long cables swung beneath the four colorful helicopters as they flitted between the drill rigs, in a constant cycle of lifting, lowering, and delivering, never seeming to pause for more than a moment. A small red plane buzzed back and forth on seemingly endless fuel runs. A half-dozen drill rigs ran day and night, interrupting the quiet darkness with beams of light and a constant mechanized humming.

But these drill rigs are pinpricks on the land—mere specks in what they aim to create. The drills pierced four thousand feet beneath us, slurping nearly three hundred gallons of fuel each day they pushed deeper. Looking for copper. Looking for gold. Looking for money. The smell of exhaust and the constant mechanical rumble provided a backdrop to our conversation.

I approached the first drill rig nervously, hanging a few paces behind the bolder Hig. I disagreed with the mine proposal. And I worried what the mine company's workers might think of me.

We introduced ourselves, as always, with our adventure. We said we'd walked from Seattle—said we were walking to the Aleutians. A small crowd of workers came out of the warming shack to snap their pictures with us. They stuck out oil-blackened work gloves to shake our hands. My grubby ski glove suddenly seemed less dirty than it would in a village. Everyone was smiling.

I talked adventure with a hard-hatted worker from eastern Washington, learning about the fuel consumption of drill rigs and the cost of helicopters as I talked about the gorgeous views from the mountains. He reminisced about the "olden days" at the Pebble site, before stricter standard operating procedures, when it was possible to get dropped on a peak by one of those helicopters—just to see the world. It reminded me of our stay in the mining camp back at Sulphurets Creek. These workers were adventurers too.

But the workers couldn't change the basic equation of the project. What once was a mountain might become a vast pile of toxic waste, requiring careful containment for years, generations, and centuries. In this process, things often go wrong. If they go wrong here, Bristol Bay's extraordinary fish resources—along with the 320-million-dollar fishery, the residents, and the wildlife that depend on them—are at risk.

13. WINTER STORMS, WINTER SUN

Letter from a Nondalton student:
"I don't think I would walk that far, because
I don't want to be dirty and stinky. But who
knows, I might change my mind."

FIFTEEN KIDS—the entirety of Iliamna's Newhalen elementary school—clustered around us in a tight circle on the floor of the classroom, shouting out a barrage of rapid-fire questions as we pulled hiking gear out of our packs.

"Are you scared sleeping outside?"

"No. What would we be...?"

"You're married?"

"Yes, we got married in..."

"How old are you?"

"Well, I'm twenty-eight, and Hig's thirty-one."

"What do you eat?"

"We eat a lot of different things, mostly stuff that has lots of fat and not much water..."

"Do you need to have good grades to go on a trip like this?"

"Umm... Education is important, because we need to do a lot of planning, and writing..."

I hated to tell a kid he didn't need good grades. And it was true we used skills from our education all the time. But expedition sponsors don't scrutinize report cards. And it wasn't likely he'd learn wilderness skills in class.

Our shelter—mostly buried under a snowdrift in McNeil Pass, Katmai National Park

The teachers hung back around the edge of the carpeted room, recording the encounter in the flashes and clicks of pocket cameras. Five different kids held the five different pieces of our kayak paddle, and I tried to orchestrate its assembly. I barely had time to half-answer each question before I was hit with the next.

"How come you have these funny things on your shoes?"

"They're called ski-boot tongues. They're for attaching to the skis. See, the pins on the toe stick into... Hold on a second. You've got the middle of the paddle, see..."

"Have you seen any wolves?"

"Yes, but not for a while. Wolves usually..."

"Do you have any kids?"

"Not yet. We couldn't leave them behind for a year if we did! Umm, I think the kid in the green shirt has the piece of paddle we need now..."

"How come you don't have a real house?"

"It would be too heavy! If we had a real house..."

I finally corralled all the paddle pieces into a coherent whole, and passed them to Hig, who was directing another handful of kids in attaching the ties of our shelter to the classroom desks.

"How do you wash? Do you wash in the lakes?"

I turned to the little girl who had asked the question, thankful that I'd been able to both shower and wash clothes in Iliamna before we hit the school.

"Not when it's winter. The lakes are frozen!"

As I said it, I thought to myself that we almost never wash in lakes even in the summer. The lakes are still cold, and hot weather is rare in this part of the world. We're used to dirt, and taking the effort to get clean rarely seems to be worth it. We could be traveling, or taking photographs, or repairing broken gear...

"Well, how do you wash, then?" she asked.

"We borrow showers from nice folks when we get to towns," I replied, thinking I might take another soon.

Sweat was beading up on my face, and I'd already stripped down as much as I could. We were well equipped for frigid winter snowstorms, but didn't have a stitch of clothing appropriate for the great indoors.

"How often is that?"

I shrugged. "It depends on how far apart the towns are."

The little girl gave me a quizzical look, clearly unsure what to make of an adult woman so unconcerned with personal hygiene. I looked down at myself. The dark-brown top of my homemade fleece long underwear was misshapen and baggy. Little bits of plastic peeled from the knee and butt patches on my black dry suit pants. Tears on the legs had been stitched with white dental floss, and goobered over with messy globs of waterproof glue. My ski boots were muddy from the bicycle ride across town. The expedition had long since demolished my last tatters of self-consciousness, but I did wonder what on earth we must have looked like to those village kids.

We talked to kids in the schools along the way whenever we got a chance. I tell myself that we taught them a little about the natural world around them, and how it connects to places farther away. I tell myself we might have inspired a few of them to explore the wild country surrounding their homes.

But let's be honest: We were the traveling freak show—little more, perhaps, than an amusing break from ordinary classes. Maybe we taught them that only oddballs go hiking. Or maybe we provided an example of a different (bizarre, entertaining, ridiculous, unheard of) way to be an adult.

• • •

Another of our winding detours brought us across the frozen Lake Iliamna, past Pedro Bay village, to the pass between Pile Bay and Iliamna Bay. Our eventual goal lay southwest down the spine of the Alaska Peninsula. Instead, we went east, and were now climbing over another pass to return to Cook Inlet. One rationale was to follow the general route the mine road would take if Pebble is built. Our other rationale was sheer enjoyment. As we headed down the Alaska Peninsula, our route zigzagged between three distinct regions: the Pacific coast, the Bering Sea coast, and the lakes and tundra between them. We wanted to see it all.

Just below the pass, I took off my left glove, fished out a pair of wrapped caramels, and handed one to Hig. The warmth of my palm had turned the hard frozen lump to a soft sticky goo, and I popped it into my mouth, relishing its juicy sweetness. It was the best thing in the world. I contemplated warming up another, but we only had one bag, and I wanted to savor them. Hig chewed his absentmindedly, examining his boot.

"I think we have to stop and fix it."

It was Easter morning, about ten degrees and clear. Just past the spring equinox, a bright March sun made the whole landscape glow a blinding white. I was excited to be gliding across all this glorious snow, and felt more than ready to charge forward over the pass. Couldn't this happen during one of the storms? But looking down at Hig's ski boot, I had to nod my glum agreement. A huge crack stretched around the front of the toe, and it looked as though the whole sole might peel off if we didn't do anything.

Scattered spruce poked above the snow, and we dumped our gear near the grey skeleton of a dead tree that would provide plenty of wood for a fire. It was too cold for glue to cure without some heat. With only one boot, Hig couldn't do much but sit by the fire and cook lunch, so I wandered off to take photographs.

Crossing over each other, and then over each other again, a network of ptarmigan tracks laced the snow. The prints told a story. First I'd see just the faintest fan of scratches in the snow. A few steps farther would be heavy wing-prints. After that, a short trough in the snow showed where the ptarmigan approached its final landing, its extended claws scratching through the snow. Finally, a groove of triangular, inward-turning tracks shuffled off to the nearest bush.

Looking up, I saw white blobs perched on the bare branches of half-buried alder. A flock of forty or fifty ptarmigan erupted from the nearby hillside, flashing white in front of the dark triangles of spruce trees, barely visible against the bright white snow. They let out a chorus of chuckling grunting trills, like a flock of giggling chickens.

I looped back to Hig, grabbing my half of the lunch as I told him about the birds. The ski boot was glued and drying, nearly half a tube of waterproof glue slimed across the toe. I poked the still-sticky goo.

"You know, we should make all our gear straight out of this glue. It seems to last better than any other material, and it would save us time on repairs."

I leaned on my ski pole—broken in half and splinted. Our big orange dry bag was torn, and only half repaired. The fabric of my backpack was laced with tiny tears, and I packed things gingerly to avoid expanding them. Hig's other ski boot threatened to rip apart any day, and we resolved to take it to bed with us in the hopes we could warm it up enough to glue without having to waste half a day around the fire making repairs. This was Hig's second pair of ski boots. I was on my third.

Everything falls apart. We had done our best to resupply in Anchorage. We had repaired everything while we were there. And that wasn't even two months ago. First, one sleeping pad failed beyond what we could repair. And then my second pair of ski boots did the same. It seemed as though we had to order something new in every village, getting it mailed to the next stop along our route, and making do with the broken version for the week or two it took our skiing to coordinate with online retailers and the postal service. Glue, needles, and dental floss (serving as thread) became our prize possessions.

· · ·

Our journey had morphed from a nine-month plan to a year-long reality. Half of that delay was storms and ice and darkness—beginning on the Lost Coast, and smacking down our best-laid plans with the harsh truth of an Alaskan winter. The other half was people.

Our schedule crumbled, and we found that our priorities had shifted. As fall slid into winter, we had begun to dawdle in towns and villages, taking more time for visits, for slideshows, and for chats with the school kids. And we saw no reason to hurry. The longer we traveled, the more we would get to see of spring. There was something that seemed special about traveling for a whole year. The more I thought about it, the more I decided that a year would be just right. Hadn't I told Hig years ago, long before we had any sort of plan, that I wanted to journey through all four seasons? So we redrew our line, adding detours to scenery and detours to visit towns, allowing more time to linger in each community. We had as much to learn from the people as we did from the natural world around them.

So after only a day on the Pacific coast, we continued our zigzag, turning west from Iliamna Bay, back to Lake Iliamna and the town of Kokhanok.

My first hot shower was like a burst of liquid gold. Clean hair distracted me, and I ran my fingers through the silky strands. No longer held in place with grease or a hood, wisps fell into my eyes, and I brushed them away, wondering where the pocketknife was. I wanted Hig to cut my bangs off again, but our possessions were scattered over every surface of the small apartment, melting and drying. Freed from its confinement, the volume of gear we managed to stuff into our dry bags and small backpacks amazed me. Indoors, in the one place the region's ever-present wind couldn't touch, it looked as if a storm had come through.

We were ensconced in Kokhanok's "Itinerant Teacher" housing—a bare apartment in a cluster of blue buildings, in the fenced-in yard of the school. All the teachers lived in this school-owned housing. Many were young, white, and new arrivals. The native man we'd met as we first set foot in town had joked about the fenced yard. Was it to keep the natives out, or to keep the white folks in? None of the locals appeared as we joined the teachers for dinner and cribbage, making plans to visit the students in the morning. The school compound really was a separate world—a village within a village.

• • •

In 1971, the Alaska Native Claims Settlement Act resolved indigenous land claims across the state through the formation of native corporations. Two hundred village corporations were formed, and then further organized into twelve regional corporations—each of which represented a large swath of the state. Forty-four million acres of land and 963 million dollars were divided among them. Native people became not landowners, but shareholders.

In Kokhanok, we stumbled upon the annual meeting of the Alaska Peninsula Corporation, a merger of five different village corporations in the region.

I picked up the hamburger from my paper plate, eating like the always-ravenous hiker I was. Most of the village residents were arranged on the bleachers around us, eating their own plates of food. Small children ran back and forth on the slippery floor of the gym. In the middle, sitting at a row of long tables, a handful of men and women slowly proceeded through the meeting.

Many of the people on the bleachers were shareholders. But not all of them. Only people alive in 1971 received those original shares. And since 1991, shares in native corporations have been open to be bought and sold by anyone, to anyone, just like the shares of any corporation.

They'd invited speakers from the Pebble Limited Partnership, who gave a progress report on the past year's exploration efforts at Pebble valley. Representatives from smaller mining companies came next, with only sketchy plans of what they hoped to accomplish in the region. Most of the crowd gave no indication of their opinions. Some approved. Some grumbled. Others gave angry tirades, asking their board of directors how to stop these projects.

While mining company representatives had been absent at the meeting in Nondalton, here they made up a majority of the invited speakers. Individual opinions varied, but each village in the Lake Iliamna and Bristol Bay regions had staked out its own position on the Pebble project. Some, like Nondalton, were unabashedly anti-mine. Others claimed neutrality, but were accused by their neighbors of being in the mining company's pocket. The Alaska Peninsula Corporation was officially neutral. The official positions of the native corporations often differed from the official positions taken by tribal or city councils—despite the fact that they supposedly represented the same people. As we traveled through the region, people on both sides of the issue lamented the discord that Pebble had caused.

• • •

We loaded our packs with a fresh batch of food, followed the gravel road past Kokhanok's airport, and walked into three solid days of storms, sleet, and eyeball-piercing rain. Each morning, I wondered what reason I could possibly have to leave our shelter. I wondered why I should get up to walk into blinding rain and sleet over snowless tundra, to lean into a gale with my heavy pack while the wind whipped the cumbersome and useless skis strapped to the top. Was it worth all this just to make a few miserable miles of progress? I wondered why we had chosen to detour again—to revisit the Pacific coast. I wondered why we had ever left Kokhanok. But each morning, I told myself that no weather lasts forever. It was the curse and the blessing of a year-long journey—a year's worth of weather.

• • •

The storm was gone. We unpeeled our bulky clothes and basked in a bright April sun. The mountains around us shook off their clouds, glowing against the blue-white sky. The perfect white cone of Augustine volcano appeared—an island in the calm waters of Kamishak Bay. Up and down the coast, impressive headlands jutted like fortress walls. Snowmelt waterfalls poured curtains of rain from overhung cliff tops. Water ran in rivulets through the cobbles, pooling in low spots in the brown tundra. Marshes resounded with the trilling clucks of ptarmigan. They flew in flocks of hundreds, leaving triangular footprints on every square inch of ground.

We needed the beautiful day. We needed the bright warm sun, the picturesque snow-frosted boulders, and the nearby peaks slowly emerging from the clouds. We needed the gentle roll of the swell, and the slip of our skis on wet hard snow as we whizzed down a slope. In short, we needed a day when anyone would have wanted to switch places with us.

• • •

Each time we visited civilization, we were peppered with questions about our daily routine from people who couldn't fathom what our lives must be like. After several instances of answering the question "How long does it take to set up camp?" with wild guesses or shrugs, we decided to find out. Night found us half a mile inland from McNeil Bay—ten miles down the coast from where we'd reached the ocean. As darkness set in, we chose a campsite. We dumped our backpacks in a pile, skiing around for a few minutes as we called back and forth to each other about the flatness, wind protection, and roominess of the spots we were investigating. My journal lay open next to the backpacks, pencil clipped to an open page which I gradually filled with a column of numbers.

8:38 — We pick the spot, start gathering firewood.
We were on a gentle slope of half-buried alders. The three-foot brush would provide decent wind protection, and we'd found a bare patch of snow with a large enough footprint to easily fit the shelter. We left the ski poles with our packs, stomping around awkwardly in the skis as we carried armfuls of dead branches for the evening's fire.

8:47 — We finish collecting firewood. Erin goes to work on the shelter while Hig starts cooking.
Wordlessly, we each picked up our standard tasks, moving with practiced efficiency. Hig called out to me every few minutes, and I wrote down the times for each phase of his cooking as I arranged the yellow and grey pyramid neatly on the snow.

8:51 — Hig has the fire started.

8:54 — Hig puts a pot of snow on the fire.

8:58 — Erin has the stakes (skis) set for the four corners of the shelter.
I liked setting up the shelter. I fussed with the placement of the skis and the tightness of each tie until each silnylon panel was crisp and taut. I stood back to view the results, pleased with the neatness of the perfect pyramid.

9:14 — Erin has the bed spot stomped down in the shelter.

9:07 — Erin has the pole (paddle) set, and the shelter corners square. Shelter is up.

9:25 — Hig has a hot drink ready, passes it to Erin, and adds new snow to the pot.
Hot pomegranate tea steamed in my titanium mug, which I balanced on a folded-up dry bag so it wouldn't chill too quickly on the snow. I carefully brushed snow off the thin piece of foam that served as the floor of our bed, arranging the many layers that allowed skinny hairless humans to sleep in this harsh world. Deflated rafts. Foam pad. Inflatable sleeping pads. Homemade synthetic sleeping bag. Homemade down quilt arranged inside the bag. Why couldn't we just bury ourselves in the snow like the wolves or the ptarmigan?

9:25 — Erin has sleeping pads and bags spread out for the bed.

9:31 — Erin is arranging the rest of the gear.

9:40 — Erin is snuggled into bed.
I jumped into bed first, as I often do, warming it up for Hig and arranging the last of our stuff.

9:50 — Erin finds and switches dead headlamp batteries for live ones.

9:55 — Hig has dinner ready.
Hig handed me a steaming pot of spaghetti, butter, and cheese. Cheesy noodles are our absolute favorite hiking food, and I devoured them greedily, aiming to eat as close to exactly half as I could. Hig stayed outside. I like crawling into bed to get a start on my writing. Hig likes messing with the fire. I like my food as hot as it can be without actually burning me. Hig likes it cooler. Our system worked perfectly. I licked the cheese from the spoon, feeling lucky and contented.

10:02 — Erin finishes eating her portion; Hig finishes adjusting the middle ties on the shelter.

10:05 — Hig finishes his dinner; Erin is writing in journal.

10:10 — Hig gets into bed.

10:16 — Hig is snuggled into bed, goes to sleep.
The last piece of every day is always mine alone. Scratching with a pencil in my waterproof notebook, I wrote, trying to keep as much of me inside the warm bag as possible. Hig snored gently beside me, and I tried not to elbow him in my wriggling.

10:46 — Erin finishes writing in the journal, goes to sleep.
This night, it only took me a half hour to finish my reflections. Often it was longer. Finally I switched off my headlamp, hung it on the paddle supporting our shelter for easy reach in the night, and curled up against Hig, only my face exposed to the chill air. A perfect routine.

. . .

The next day, the snow fell thicker and thicker, creeping in to surround us in its opaque blanket. I gazed around, compass in hand, trying to assure myself we were still heading toward the pass. All the world was a pure, blank, impenetrable white. It was enough to make my eyes hurt. I closed them, giving myself a few seconds of darkness for variety. Open or closed, there was nothing to see.

White surrounded me. No line or shadow marked where snow in the air met snow on the ground. I was skiing on the sky. I could hear the swish of powder beneath my skis. I stared at their bright blue tips, spots of color in the featureless white.

A stiff breeze swirled in from behind us, piling snow on our packs. I barely noticed it. For more than half a year, wind had been our nearly constant companion, and this day was no different....

Until, suddenly, it stopped. We were nearly bowled over by the abrupt lack of wind, by the unexpected wall of quiet.

. . .

On the base of the Alaska Peninsula, we were trapped between the warring weather patterns of two massive bodies of water, the Pacific Ocean and the Bering Sea. Wet, warm air from Pacific high pressure zones races west across the peninsula, rushing out over the Bering Sea. From Bering highs, arctic winds blast the other way. We were standing in McNeil Pass, the steep mountains surrounding us angled just right to funnel the wind between the seas.

It was as though someone was trying to even the levels in two pitchers of water, pouring too much from the Pacific pitcher into the Bering container, pausing for a moment to check the levels, then quickly pouring the water back the other way. We were right in the spout.

The moment's pause was over. In less than half an hour, the wind had shifted 180 degrees, pouring in from the Bering Sea and growing stronger by the minute. Streams of powder began to lift from the ground. Snowflakes flew, stinging my eyes with every crystalline speck. Each gust sent curls of snow into the air, buffeting us as we skied against them.

Darkness fell quickly. Hunched behind a pair of boulders, we donned our last spare scraps of clothing, bundling up as much as possible while swirling eddies screamed around us.

We built a wall. Hig worked quickly with the blade of the kayak paddle, cutting irregular snow blocks and stacking them like giant bricks. I crouched behind the wall, gathering handfuls of powder snow and packing them between my mittened hands to chink the cracks between the snow blocks. Wind whistled through every gap, sending swirls of blowing snow into the island of calm we were struggling to create.

After an hour of work, my fingers and toes were freezing. But we had a snow fort any child would be proud of—a wall six feet tall and eight feet long to ward off the brunt of the wind, with two smaller walls wrapping around each side. With no wood for a fire and no hope of a hot meal, we moved straight into setting up the shelter. The task seemed agonizingly slow, even with both of us working. I snapped crankily at Hig, then immediately apologized and gave him a hug. Griping at Hig was just as effective as griping at the wind—momentarily satisfying, but utterly useless.

Working together, we set ties on opposite sides of the shelter, driving the skis deep into the snow. Even behind the snow wall, the sides of shelter beat and billowed in the wind, making sharp cracking sounds that made me think the whole thing was about to tear apart. We tried to bury the edges in piles of snow, but it was a hopeless proposition. Fine and light as mist, the snow seemed to fill the whole volume of our little home, drifting and swirling, settling like dust. I hurried my evening journal writing, pencil gripped awkwardly in a cold, gloved hand, listening to the roar.

Hours later in the darkness, I mumbled sleepily at Hig as he tried to explain why we needed to switch the direction of our feet and heads. Something about snow, and tearing walls, and suffocation… I was warm, comfortable, and not keen on moving anywhere. He insisted. I woke up enough to notice that a huge mass of snow was piled on the outside of our shelter, hanging mere inches over my nose. If the fabric collapsed, we needed a way to dig ourselves out. We shrunk into the tiny clear space by the pole in the middle, awkwardly squirming into a new position. I tucked myself into our poofy black sleeping bag, ignoring the swirls of snow still blowing through the tiny cracks, ignoring the raging howls of the storm outside, and quickly returned to a cozy sleep.

. . .

Those big snowdrifts you find behind rocks in snowy mountain passes? They don't take nearly as long to accumulate as you might think. Our snow wall protected us from the brunt of the wind. But it formed a perfect snow fence to catch a drift behind it.

All through the night, the thin nylon walls of our pyramid sagged inward under an ever-increasing load of blowing snow. As the storm progressed, the snow bowed the sides of our shelter further and further in, burying gear we'd left at the outer edges.

The next morning, the snow-free peak of our pyramid allowed some light from the bright, clear sky above, but most of our shelter was dark. In fact, most of our shelter was simply missing—walls pressed flat to the ground by a giant drift.

"I can't believe we slept a full night!" Hig exclaimed. "With the wind roaring, in this claustrophobic space, being buried by snow…"

"Well, these conditions don't really make you want to get going early."

I could hear the wind still roaring and wasn't in any hurry to extricate myself from our cramped but warm space. I kept my hood pulled tight around my face, munching on Grape Nuts. Hig extracted the video camera, describing our predicament to some hypothetical audience.

"Can you help me find my sock?"

I grumbled. "Mmmph…still eating…still waking up…"

"I just want to get out of here. I'm worried the shelter will collapse, and I want to start shoveling."

"It held all night. What are the chances that right now is the critical moment?"

Hig went first, video camera in hand. While I was putting my boots on, the shelter collapsed. The weight of the snow sent our paddle pole punching straight through the roof. No longer a small tent, it was now a small doghouse and my second boot lay buried somewhere beneath the snow.

"I found a cooking vessel!" Hig cried a half-hour later, holding up our blackened cook pot.

"Can you tell by its decorations what sort of culture it originated from?" I deadpanned.

"It must have been an impoverished culture…only soot blackening on this dented aluminum pot."

Half a kayak paddle in my mittened hands, I shoveled snow off another corner of our flattened shelter. Retrieving our buried gear, we felt as though we were performing archaeology on ourselves.

The world was harsh but grand. Sun lit the wind-sculpted snow in our bare mountain pass. A knee-deep river of spindrift snow ran along the ground just above it. Clouds flew by overhead, blinking the sun and shadows on and off. Gusts lifted the river from the ground, sending plumes and walls of snow hurtling through the air, suddenly whiting out our world.

· · ·

As we dropped out of the pass, the wind died. The shift in weather had brought us cold clear air and a brilliant sun that would carry us all the way to our next rendezvous with civilization.

"Look, that ptarmigan's got a dark head!" Hig called out, pointing at a bizarre-looking bird with a mottled brown head on a snow-white body.

"A mutant!"

"Maybe it's just changing…"

"Oh yeah," I laughed at my silliness. "It's changing for spring."

We were approaching the middle of April. Already, we had twice as much daylight as we'd seen in the depths of December's darkness. The spring sun swept over us, high in the sky, melting the world with its blazing power.

We descended toward the Bering Sea, through the frozen lakes and rolling tundra of Katmai National Park. Each night, the world froze. Frost formed quickly on our fur ruffs, and we bundled up as thoroughly as we had in December, grateful for every scrap of winter insulation. Each day, the world melted. We stripped off layers of clothing, basking in the warmth.

We skied, then ski-walked, and finally walked, traveling over spongy moss on thawing bear trails. We snacked on the newly thawed remains of last year's cranberries as we walked on soggy piles of last year's cottonwood leaves.

Our sun block froze solid in its tube overnight, and our noses and lips began to turn red. We flew across the lakes of Katmai Park—still solid sheets of blazing white. One pair of sunglasses was lost. Hig turned his balaclava backwards, trying to protect his eyes by looking out through the smallest of peepholes. One ski pole was broken. I pushed myself ahead with the remaining pole.

Grosvenor Lake thrummed beneath our feet—a deep booming gurgle that pounded and echoed. Occasionally the booms were followed by the unnerving sound of a long, slow cracking, as if the lake was about to part beneath us in one accelerated thaw. Even with sunglasses, I squinted, one eye shut and the other watering, trying to distinguish islands from ridges, and pressure cracks from lines of wolverine tracks. Sometimes I closed my eyes entirely, focusing on the graceful speed of skiing, the warm sun on my back, the sense of gliding across the land.

The weather was glorious, but it left Hig mostly snow-blind, seeing the gorgeous landscape in a bleary double vision. We were almost out of food, but we were almost to the next spot where food could be found.

In a bright orange sunset, two trumpeter swans took off from a small pool of open water on Naknek Lake. They were the first migratory birds we'd seen since November. I was excited for spring.

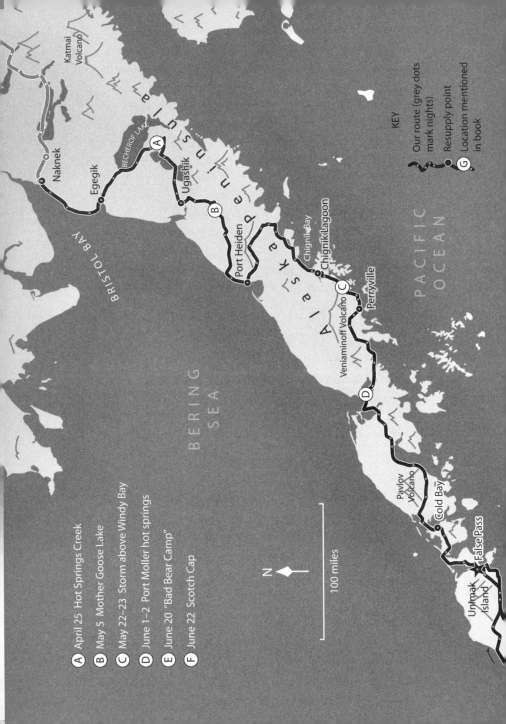

KEY

Our route (grey dots mark nights)

● Resupply point

Ⓖ Location mentioned in book

Katmai Volcano

Naknek

Egegik

BECHAROF LAKE

Ⓐ

Ugashik

Ⓑ

Port Heiden

Chignik Bay

Chignik Lagoon

Ⓒ

Perryville

Veniaminof Volcano

Ⓓ

Pavlov Volcano

Cold Bay

False Pass

Unimak Island

Alaska Peninsula

BRISTOL BAY

BERING SEA

PACIFIC OCEAN

N

100 miles

Ⓐ April 25 Hot Springs Creek
Ⓑ May 5 Mother Goose Lake
Ⓒ May 22–23 Storm above Windy Bay
Ⓓ June 1–2 Port Moller hot springs
Ⓔ June 20 "Bad Bear Camp"
Ⓕ June 22 Scotch Cap

SPRING

[APRIL 15–JUNE 27]

897 MILES

14. BERING SEA SLEEPING

Erin: "Imagine what we could do with a heated building
that we didn't have to move out of every day?"

I HELD THE VIDEO CAMERA just above the ground, lens trained on Hig's
mud-spattered ski boots. Each step brought his tractionless sole down
through a thin layer of gooey mud, spread like grease over a platform of
melting ice.

It was the middle of April. The bluffs above the Bering Sea were swept
bare of snow—golden grasses and red-brown tundra broken only by a few
small patches of brush. Small piles of white feathers clung to depressions
and waved in the wind, evidence of molting ptarmigan. We'd abandoned
our skis in Naknek. But our trail-running shoes were still winging their way
through the mail to our next stop in the town of Egegik. I'd borrowed some
boots from our Naknek host, but Hig still walked in his ski boots.

We walked the tundra. We walked muddy beaches. We walked on ice.
Jumbled sea ice swirled in the strong tidal currents of Bristol Bay, shearing into smaller and smaller pieces. When the tide dropped, ice pans rested
askew on the infinite mudflats. When the tide came in, dirty white ice
covered the water to a distant horizon. Plates of broken ice piled on the
beaches, bridging tiny streams and winding sloughs. Dirt showered from
the crumbling bluffs above and mixed with the melting ice to transform the
shore into an oozing, slippery mess.

Old wooden fishing boats are overgrown with grass and shrubs near an abandoned
cannery in South Naknek on the Bering Sea coast.

Occasionally we spotted old cabins perched on the cliff tops, silhouetted against the grey sky. They leaned and crumbled. Their walls were broken open as if the wind had hit them with the force of an explosion. They clung precariously to a shrinking world, tumbling over the edge as the ground fell away beneath them.

From below, I could view the cabin floors where they hung over open air. From above, I gazed at the trails weaving between them. Parallel ruts left by the tires of four-wheelers, they snaked along until they disappeared over the edge.

Actually, the cabins weren't that old. But they stood in the brunt of the Bering Sea's harsh weather, on the edge of a quickly shrinking coastline. Storms and tides lapped at the base of the soft bluffs, leaving mats of woven tundra hanging and flapping from their upper edges. As the world warms and the storms on this windswept edge grow larger, erosion will speed up with them. Waves crash against the base of the bluffs, and every year the Bering Sea claims a bigger bite of the land.

. . .

The canneries slept. Battened down for the winter, a cluster of mint-green wooden buildings creaked and groaned in the wind. An old metal fan sat discarded among piles of rusting clutter, whirling steadily on the grass. We stepped carefully over the downed power line that lay across the gravel path, looking for signs of life.

Egegik lay on the far side of the river. We followed the rutted four-wheeler tracks cautiously across the ice, aware that even though the machine that had left them was heavier than either of us, several days of melting had passed since the tracks were laid down. I stayed well apart from Hig, both of us watching the ice carefully as we traversed the mile-wide expanse of the Egegik River. Like a yellow tail, my empty packraft swished over the ice behind me. It wasn't really a sled—it was my emergency lifeboat. But the ice stayed solid. For a little longer, we were on the right side of breakup.

Egegik itself was hardly more alive than the boarded-up canneries across the river—a complex of buildings, docks, and containers that swallowed the few dozen winter residents. In June, the human population would increase fifty-fold or more, from a few dozen souls to cannery barracks stuffed with thousands. Every other town on the coast would do the same. The jumbled floes of ice in the bay would be replaced by a jumbled fleet of fishing boats. The bears would shake off their winter slumber to return to the riverbanks. And the salmon would return.

Millions of salmon. Tens of millions of salmon. The frozen lakes we'd been skiing over since Lake Clark rear sockeye salmon in overwhelming abundance. Our hosts in Naknek fed their two huge sled dogs mainly on wild salmon—bags of dog food were too expensive. In this corner of the world, there was plenty of salmon for all.

If state regulators manage things properly, perhaps there will always be enough salmon. Regulators can't control the state of the ocean—its pollution or temperature or the acid formed from dissolved carbon dioxide. But in this corner of the Bering Sea, they can manage the harvest and keep spawning rivers pristine. The salmon fishery is an industry that might be sustainable for generations to come.

• • •

I bent down to look closely at the muddy beach, examining the fresh imprint of a wolverine's paw, left only a minute earlier by the dark, loping shape we'd seen running along the base of the bluffs.

"Bear!"

I startled at Hig's cry, my heart beginning to pound. I scanned the beach, eyes flicking back and forth in search of a furry brown form. It had to be close. My hand strayed to the can of pepper spray. Nothing. I turned my worried gaze to Hig.

"First one of the season!" he continued, gleefully.

Puzzled, I followed the line of his eyes down to the mud. There, each toeprint filled with a tiny puddle of water, was the clear impression of a bear's front foot. The print was obviously older than the wolverine tracks I'd just been examining and older than the last high tide.

"Don't say it like that!" I admonished. "Yelling 'Bear!' when you're looking at a track."

"I'm sorry," he apologized sheepishly. "I was excited."

But that track had been laid in the last few days. At least one of the peninsula's bears was awake.

. . .

No longer the solid sheet we'd crossed just a few days before, the candle ice on the Egegik River crumbled with a soft tinkling hiss. Golden sun shone on the icy golden marsh, where seagulls wheeled overhead, screeching and screaming. It felt as though years had passed since we'd heard that song. The temperature was barely above freezing, but I could almost believe it was a warm summer day at the beach. Almost.

Newly nimble in trail-running shoes, I balanced on a frozen lump of sod, trying to give my poor feet a moment's break from the pools of ice water. Sandhill cranes strode through the ponds around us, their continual stuttering cry like a wet finger squeaking on glass: *"I'm a crane! I'm a crane! I'm a crane!"* Gangly awkward dinosaurs of the bird world, they rose up in funny hopping twirls—mating dances.

At 10 PM, I sat in our tent, writing by the light of the newly lengthened day. Outside, the land honked, moaned, squeaked, cried, and chirped in a cacophony of birdsong.

. . .

From the Egegik River, we turned inland again, following the frozen edges of lakes at the foothills of volcanoes. Large, textured crystals made the ice of Becharof Lake as grippy as a sidewalk. Miles flew by quickly, but each was the same as the last. The hard ice set my feet to aching. And as we left the marshes behind, the bird songs disappeared with them.

Seven years prior, we had walked the lush green shores of Becharof Lake under August skies, wading streams choked with splashing red salmon and weaving through crowds of bears. That two-month journey down the Alaska Peninsula had been our first expedition—inspiration for everything that followed. I tried to remember how this area looked on that trip, remembering it as one of the most alive places I'd ever seen. Now, under an overcast April sky, all seemed bleak and dead.

But the volcanoes brought us scenery impervious to the seasons. Just beyond the edge of the lake, deep craters appeared in the tundra. The chasms were incongruous in the gently rolling landscape—the misplaced eruption of a nearby volcano. Hig skated down the steep scree slope at the edge of a crater, exploring the frozen lake at its bottom, while I photographed him from the rim. Beyond the craters, we left the melting tundra behind and climbed back into the snow on the flanks of Ugashik Caldera.

Tiny streams of bubbles rose from the pools of Hot Springs Creek. Its rocks were coated with a bright decoration of slimy green and orange-red algae. I took my hand from its mitten, dipping my fingers in lukewarm water, and bringing them up to my mouth. The drops left a sharp sulfurous tang on my tongue.

Caribou droppings were scattered on the creek's grassy banks, where they had come to take advantage of this tiny oasis. Even in the depths of winter, the heat of the water kept the plants uncovered—a green spot in a world of snow. We followed the bubbling pools and trickles, testing the warmth every few feet, hoping for something hotter. Finally, our shoes still on, we waded into an ankle-deep pool of frothing hot water. Its warmth displaced the slush-cold wetness we'd grown used to against our feet. Shiny black sand bubbled from its depths.

It wasn't quite the hot bath I had hoped for. But it was a spot of wonder. We dropped a pair of frozen candy bars into the water, watching them spin in the stream of bubbles while we warmed our feet, crouching behind a boulder to hide from the stinging chill of blowing snow.

• • •

As we walked, we talked and daydreamed, transporting our minds ahead to some kind of future. We weren't sure exactly when it would happen, but in a couple months we would reach the end of our road, on the southwestern tip of Unimak Island. And from there?

"I think spending a year in the wilderness changes your perspective on how you want to live," I mused. "Before, when we lived in Seattle, I thought it was wonderful to have a Trader Joe's store within walking distance. I was so used to being surrounded by everything we might want or need: dozens of restaurants, movies, an aikido dojo, all the kinds of stores we could imagine. Now I find myself thinking: 'Imagine what we could do with a heated building that we didn't have to move out of every day?'"

Hig laughed. "I guess after this, pretty much anything is going to be moving up in the world, huh?"

When the conveniences of the city surround you, it's hard to imagine giving them up. But when they're thousands of miles away, you have a chance to reexamine your assumptions. You begin to wonder if you really need so much. By giving all that up, we could start building a life from scratch, assembling the pieces that really mattered.

Hig began to call our journey a "scouting trip for life." We'd left Seattle without knowing where our next home would be. Everything we'd left behind faded into memory, until we could hardly recall why we owned any boxes of stuff we weren't carrying, and what those boxes might contain. Living surrounded by mountains and snow, I had long since ceased thinking about movie theaters and restaurants. And with each person we visited, we studied his or her life, wondering what might work for our own.

It wasn't long after we entered Alaska that we knew we would find some way to stay. Maybe we would find jobs in Anchorage or Juneau—recreating our old lives somewhere closer to the wilderness. But the long months of fall and winter had brought us beyond that obvious vision, into a plan far more stripped-down than we might have ever imagined. As we were welcomed by tiny community after tiny community, I wondered what it would be like to live there, or somewhere equally small. Without even realizing it, our future had changed.

15. AWAKENING

*Hig: "I don't think the ears grow as much as
the rest of the bear. So when you see really small ears,
that means it's a really big bear."*

WE WENT TO SLEEP in the rain. The next morning, I opened my eyes, peering under the slightly sagging walls at a world turned white with snow. And then I closed them again. The hissing on our shelter said it was still snowing, and it looked as though several inches had fallen. We'd gone to bed early, but still we slept longer. Slept late. Slept as if we might take a cue from the bears and wait until it was really spring to emerge from our den. I wondered if it was the last time snow would fall on us. Sometime, someday, the world would have to warm up again.

A few hours later, I was submerged to my ankles in icy water, jabbing my walking stick into the pond for stability. The muddy pile of sticks sunk and swayed beneath me like a bridge of Jell-O. Fat white snowflakes fluttered onto the beaver dam, coating the pieces above water with a fluffy white.

"So spring," I said sarcastically, "is the season where it's snowing on you, but you have to wade through the icy streams instead of skiing across them?"

"That's right," Hig smiled, filming my precarious traverse.

We paused on another frozen pond, catching sight of a small furry form. Two hops and a slide, a hop, and another long slide—the arched brown body of the river otter flattened on the ice, shooting across the pond

*Following the tracks of a very large bear after a close encounter with him in the hills
between Mother Goose Lake and Port Heiden*

like nothing so much as a high-speed slug. The belly sliding didn't look faster than the otter's run, or any more efficient. But it did look like more fun. We'd seen plenty of belly-slide tracks; now we finally could watch one of their creators in action. Perhaps we should be more patient with the weather. The otters were in no hurry for spring.

. . .

The evening sun topped each bush with golden highlights, casting long blue shadows across the lumpy ground near Mother Goose Lake. We wound through the willow brush on a narrow bear trail, feet crunching on the wet new snow.

A few feet ahead of me, Hig suddenly stopped. "Video camera!" he hissed, in an insistent whisper.

I pulled it from the little red pouch around my neck, handing it over. "I don't see anything. What is it?"

"Bear. It's coming toward us."

I heard the catch of fear in his voice, and I scrambled to grab and ready my giant can of pepper spray, discarding the bright-orange safety clip on the snow. Why hadn't he said "Bear!" first!?

With a lumbering run, the bear quickly closed the gap between us. I stood with my thumb on the lever of the pepper spray, nervously waiting. Hig had the video camera flipped open, talking into its tiny microphone.

"Our first spring bear..."

The bear slowed to a walk, circling around us as it continued to advance. The frothing drool dripping from its mouth was not encouraging.

"I know it's been a hard spring...," Hig spoke gently—this time to the bear.

I gripped the can more tightly. I'd carried pepper spray for years. Perhaps this time, I would actually have to use it. This bear wasn't just curious. This bear was hungry. Skinny, hungry, and huge. I was sure this big old boar was just out of his den. And he looked ready to toss a bear's typical caution to the winds.

"You don't want to mess with us!" I warned in a slow, deep, disapproving voice. "You don't want to do this...."

The bear continued his slow circle, peering at us from under the edge of a willow, carefully weighing whether we were food or threat. I stepped onto a handy tundra mound, slightly apart from Hig, so the pair of us might look larger. The bear started slightly.

"Yeah!" I called to him defiantly "We're big!"

Hig calls it my "Bad dog!" voice. He has a point. I try to drive a threatening bear away with the same disapproving tone I use to stop a disobedient dog from nosing in the trash.

All advice will tell you that you're supposed to talk to a bear. It lets him know you're a human. But it's kind of difficult to have a sensible conversation with someone who doesn't speak English, weighs over 1,000 pounds, has sharp-clawed paws bigger than my head, and is staring at me with drool dripping from his mouth. What should I say?

"Hello. I'm a human. And I'm holding something that will make your eyes water, so perhaps you shouldn't come over here and take a swat with those three-inch-long claws of yours."

Or, "Hello. I'm a human. And we humans have been using technology to kill you guys for generations, so you should recognize me as more than the fragile slab of meat that I might appear to be."

Or, "Hello. I'm a human. And whatever you do to me, bears that mess with humans usually don't end well, so it's not a good idea."

We spun to keep facing the bear as he circled us. He was taking his sweet time deciding what to do. I eyed landmarks around me, determining the best course of action. If the bear passed that bush, or that tuft of grass, then I'd spray. I was grateful for the lack of wind—nothing to complicate the spray's trajectory.

Suddenly, the bear turned and took a few running steps away from us. Just as suddenly, he changed his mind, spinning around to resume his circling approach. I held my breath, silently willing the bear's decision.

"You can go away," Hig said softly. "Leave us alone."

The bear paused, staring at us, swinging his head back and forth. Long seconds passed, and then he whirled abruptly. His huge feet kicked up sprays of snow as he ran through the bushes, and we were treated to the familiar and extraordinarily welcome sight of a galloping bear butt.

"There you go," Hig said. "Good choice. Thank you. Very much."

We continued in the direction the bear had come from, following the line of his platter-sized tracks. They were crisp and perfect in the remains of the early May snowstorm. I stuck out my foot for comparison, nearly fitting my size-eight sneaker sideways in the bear's front print.

"Wow—that's an enormous bear. Somehow it's easier to tell now, than when we were actually looking at the whole animal."

"I don't think the ears grow as much as the rest of the bear," Hig mused. "So when you see really small ears, that means it's a really big bear."

We photographed the prints, chattering with the intensity of the waning adrenaline in our blood. It was late evening already, and we kept walking right to sunset, wanting to put as much distance as possible between our camp and that bear.

I pitched the shelter in a grove of stubby cottonwoods, each one bent in the direction of the prevailing winds as if it were a blade of grass, rather than a foot-wide trunk. Orange-pink light shone through the black tangle of branches. We talked about the bear as we crawled into bed, then fell immediately into a deep, trouble-free sleep.

Our pepper spray sat by the center pole of the pyramid, still unused. Many have told us we're crazy for not carrying a gun. But a gun isn't necessarily enough to kill a giant bear instantly. Not always enough for an experienced marksman with a large rifle—much less for folks like us. Even a fatal shot might give the bear plenty of time to badly injure or kill us before he fell. But pepper spray could instantly render his senses useless. And an Alaskan researcher's study showed pepper spray came out on top. But in this encounter—and at least a hundred others we'd had over the years—it didn't matter what we carried. It didn't matter whether we carried anything at all.

It's always hard to wrap my mind around the fact that enormous bears run away from puny little humans. But almost always, they do.

• • •

The Bering Sea was liquid again. Waves gently lapped the sand, erasing a line of bear tracks as the tide rose. I kicked a rock, sending it skidding along the dark grey beach. I picked up another rock, bouncing it lightly on my palm before tossing it into the sea. White and black piles of styrofoam-light pumice formed a thick drift line at the top of the beach, tunneled and pockmarked with hundreds of small holes. From the shore, the Aniakchak volcano that had thrown them here was just a low snowy ridge, barely visible in the distance.

The fisheries here don't end with salmon. Muddy, shallow, and almost arctic, the Bering Sea is one of the richest ocean environments in the world. This is the origin of the crab in your king crab cakes and the pollock in your imitation crab sushi. Pollock from the Bering Sea makes up nearly every "fish" substance not otherwise labeled. Half the fish caught in the United States are caught here.

But warming waters are wreaking havoc with the complicated food web. As sea ice shrinks, the spring bloom of phytoplankton shrinks along with it, leaving less to eat for bottom-dwelling invertebrates, and less to eat for those larger creatures that depend on them. Walruses and seals that depend on the ice are forced into a smaller and smaller area in the north. Some species will be winners, and some will be losers. But the shift to a more temperate ecosystem threatens to strip the Bering Sea of its riches, with impacts reaching all the way to the top of the food chain—including us.

• • •

Before the United States extended its ocean borders to the two-hundred-mile limit, the Japanese fished here, catching crab in bottom-hugging nets floated with round, blown-glass balls. Scattered among more recent debris of plastic buoys and tangled nets, their floats remain.

Each glassy green-blue sphere sparkled on the field of pumice, tucked between rocks like a long-lost treasure. One was frosted by windblown sand, the next was an intense shade of green. One had barnacles growing on its surface, another was full of tiny bubbles. Others had strange indentations, streaks of blue and yellow, or odd characters stamped on the base. Each was different from the other. If they had been trinkets in a gift shop, I could have easily passed them by. But when we discovered them on the beach, they were irresistibly appealing. As we unpacked for the evening, I created a circle of glass balls—colorful and shiny on their pillow of beach grass.

"We can make a window with them," I suggested.

Loaded down under the weight of our glass-ball collection, we staggered into Port Heiden. Locals gave us tips on the best way to package them before mailing them off to Seldovia. We didn't have land, a house, or a very solid plan. But we did have the makings for a very decorative window.

. . .

"You know," I said, "it seems like all the folks we've stayed with that manage to live cheaply and flexibly in rural Alaska have three things in common: They live in small houses on their own piece of land—usually houses they built themselves. They eat a fair amount of subsistence food— from hunting, fishing, gathering, or gardening. And they heat their places with wood. So we should think about that. And we should definitely move somewhere with forests."

Hig laughed.

We mailed the glass balls to Seldovia, fairly sure that soon enough, we would follow them. We were less than two months from the end of our journey. And in some ways, Seldovia was an obvious place to start a new life. Hig had grown up in this small town on Alaska's Kenai Peninsula. His parents still lived there. Before this year-long trek, I'd never considered living in such a remote place. After all, Hig and I were modern, educated people. We were scientists, with post-secondary degrees. Moving to the 300-person village in rural Alaska where my husband grew up seemed awfully anachronistic. Seldovia wasn't even connected to the road system.

Actually, that was becoming one of its biggest selling points. Walking the shoulder of the Glenn Highway going into and out of Anchorage had soured us on the road system. We didn't want to live anywhere within the sprawling pattern of development that highways inevitably produce. As we became less and less interested in standard careers, we found ourselves less and less interested in cities that would make such careers possible. As we walked through tundra and mountains for months on end, our visions turned more and more toward rural—from a neighborhood full of conveniences to a wilderness backyard.

. . .

Tweeee Tweeee Twoooooo! Tweeee Tweeee Twoooooo! The song gave me a sudden jolt—like running into an old friend in an unexpected place. It was achingly familiar. I had been missing that sound for longer than I even remembered. Through the long months of winter, it was so easy to forget that there ever had been songbirds. In the long days of May, it was hard to remember that they'd ever been gone.

Tweeeee Tweeeee Twoooooooooo! Smaller than the palm of my hand, golden-crowned sparrows perched on the twigs at the top of every bush. Each bird stood with his tiny chest puffed out huge, quivering with the effort of making such a big noise.

Night barely touched us anymore, and it was well before dark when we pitched our pyramid in the shelter of an alder patch. I sat up in our sleeping bag, scribbling in my notebook, trying to come up with names for the birds: "Siren child" "I'm ready! I'm ready!" *"Twee. Tweedledeedee." "Hoo hoo hoo hoo hoo."* I paused, turning to Hig. "What about that one?"

We both sat silently, listening to the series of high-pitched buzzes and beeps. "That bird sounds exactly like R2D2 from *Star Wars*," he asserted.

"It does!"

We listened again, unable to keep ourselves from laughing. I added "R2D2" to the list of notes. It would be some time before we'd learn that "R2D2" is more commonly known as a fox sparrow. I didn't know the names of all the birds, but I remembered their songs. Each new arrival was an old friend returning.

. . .

At Port Heiden, we left the Bering Sea behind. Outside the village, we climbed through the snowy crater of Aniakchak volcano and began the descent to the Pacific—a month and a half since we'd last visited that ocean on Kamishak Bay. Here, where the Alaska Peninsula is only forty miles wide, it took only a few days to walk between them.

With a great *shluuuck!* sound, I pulled my foot from the thawing mountain. Masquerading as solid ground, a scattering of gravel rested loosely on a slope of pure wet mud. Gooped to the ankles, I quick-stepped to the nearest patch of tundra, trying not to lose my shoes in the muck.

The edges of the tundra turf were frayed bare and blasted white. Gusts buffeted us on the crest of the ridge. Distant lines of white caps were visible on the grey-blue expanse of the Pacific Ocean. Despite the warmth of the air, I dug out my puffy coat to insulate against the humid wind, ready to scurry down to calmer realms.

Purple! Out of the corner of my eye, I was sure I'd seen a bit of trash. I looked again, wondering how some human had managed to be in this exact remote spot to drop a bit of purple plastic on the ground.

But it wasn't trash at all. Mounds of purple mountain saxifrage flowers were scattered across the gravel scree. The tiny pincushions burst from the lifeless gravel, each perfect bloom smaller than a pencil eraser. On this unlikely, barren, and windswept ground, we cheered the first flowers of spring. We grabbed the camera back and forth from each other like eager and impatient children, lying flat on the sharp gravel slope to fill the frame with color.

Later, back in the lower-elevation brush, Hig boiled a pot of ramen soup on a fire of alder branches. I scrabbled around the matted dry grass and crumbling ferns on the river bank, looking for spring shoots. Barely an inch long, the mint green tops of pushki were still fuzzy and tightly furled. I plucked them. In a matter of minutes, the burst of new life from the ground was transformed into a burst of new green life in my mouth. I passed one to Hig, and we both broke into huge grins. I had never tasted a vegetable so fresh.

. . .

The first human tracks appeared on a plain of volcanic cinders. We'd been studying tracks for the past eleven months—the diamond-shaped prints of wolves and foxes, belly troughs of river otters slithering on snow, platter-sized bear tracks, the landing marks of a bounding rabbit, large soft-edged prints made by furry lynx feet, and the tiny shuffling trails left by mice and voles. But never boot prints.

Now there were many. The next set of boot prints formed a pair of snaking lines on the sandy beach. We followed them, weaving between washed-up logs and patches of beach grass—until one of the walkers came back to meet us.

He was a hunting guide. At his camp, we formed a circle around the skin of a recently dead bear—two guides, two hunters, and the two of us. The hide was carefully stretched on a camouflage tarp. The skull sat beside it, glistening red with still-fresh blood. Hig and I ate granola bars, drinking the tiny cans of juice the hunters offered us. All four were dressed in identical grey-green birch forest camouflage—in outfits that must have been warmer than ours. Now that we'd stopped walking, the damp chill in the air had me almost shivering. Our own camp would have had a roaring fire, and better food.

The hunters had flown in the previous week from Montana and Georgia. Soon, a plane would return to whisk them and the bear skin back to the great indoors. We would continue walking to the next village down the coast. But for now, we shared the same piece of wilderness.

From May 10 to May 25, just as the Alaska Peninsula's massive brown bears are shaking off their long winter slumber, it becomes legal to shoot them. And remote patches of wilderness that might otherwise never see a human are suddenly overrun with camouflaged outsiders crouching on bluff tops, watching the world through high-powered spotting scopes.

• • •

I've never been a hunter. I was raised a city girl in the heart of Seattle, where guns were for shooting people and wildlife sightings were rare.

But as I began making trips to Alaska, I was brought face-to-face with the concept of "wildlife as food." Seven years earlier, I found myself helping drag the still-warm carcass of a caribou onto the deck of a boat we were hitching a ride on. I tried not to look into its eyes, and I tried not to associate that life-like body with the fresh caribou heart we were served for dinner.

Wild game is part of the way people have always lived here. In a land with too-short growing seasons for most crops, fish and game are where calories come from. Wild game hunting is a way people stay connected to the land. In nearly every village, our stories of trekking were met by locals' stories of hunting—bringing us all to the same wild places, dealing with some of the same wild conditions.

But people generally don't eat brown bears. This bear's flesh was rotting where he was shot—left for the scavengers. This bear's skin would be stuffed and mounted, turned into a ferocious piece of furniture in a living room thousands of miles away. How could we support something like that?

But after over 3,500 miles of journeying, we felt differently. Both Hig and I wanted to oppose trophy hunting, but in the end, we couldn't.

In those 3,500 miles, we had seen places where the human economy and the ecosystem were thriving together. But more of the projects and development proposals we witnessed were destructive and unsustainable, many posing grave threats to communities around them—both human and natural. We had seen forests logged on a scale that wouldn't allow them to grow back, and with a thoroughness that wouldn't let any ancient forests remain. We had seen dams and fish farms that were destroying native stocks. We'd seen places where mining companies proposed to obliterate large swaths of land. All in the name of profit and jobs.

In the remote Alaska Peninsula, jobs and income are scarce. Trophy hunting brings in both—jobs and income for the guides, for the pilots, for the lodges. And unlike other money-making endeavors we'd seen, bear hunting appeared to be sustainable.

On this chunk of Pacific Coast, bears seemed to be everywhere. We followed the muddy furrows of their trails on the bluff tops, where generations of bears wore down the paths in a series of regular rounded dips, each bear stepping in the tracks of the ones that came before. Their sharp claws gouged fresh marks on the muddy slopes of gullies. We watched bears run up ridges, lumber along beaches, and walk breathtakingly steep cliff edges. We watched them grazing piles of rotten kelp, leaving piles of scat filled with chunks of pumice gravel. From all we saw ourselves or learned from others, the bear population in this region was in no threat from hunters.

As long the Alaska Department of Fish and Game sets and enforces limits that protect the bear population, trophy hunting is sustainable. It has little impact on the local landscape—most hunters leave no more trace than did Hig and I. A bear is an animal I love, but it is also a living resource—like a fish or a tree. This type of "harvesting" is not something I'll take up myself, but I don't think it's wrong.

The hunters gave us their rule of thumb for estimating the size of a bear from the size of its tracks. By their numbers, the bear that had almost charged us would have stood eleven and a half feet on his hind legs—a real prize for any hunter. I wondered if he'd been lucky enough to escape another season. When we left their camp, I wished the hunters luck. I wished the bears luck too.

. . .

Smooth black beaches arced between the rocky headlands of Chignik Bay. Craggy islands peeked out from drifting fog. Waterfalls poured from gullies in the cliffs, splashing into the surf below. The wet sand had just enough give to be easy on our feet. Flocks of tiny shorebirds ran along the drift line of clamshells and seaweed, pecking for any goodies the tide had brought in. On the dunes beside us, the sharp green shoots of rye grass were bursting through the faded tatters of pale brown stalks.

Our two lines of intertwining tracks wove their way down the beach—my unmistakable duck-footed stride, and Hig's more normal one—making small zigzags where one or the other of us deviated to snack on a patch of fresh beach greens, or to pluck a yellow agate from the sand.

"I was trying to think of reasons we shouldn't have a kid," Hig said, picking up a previous discussion. "And all that I can think of boils down to being afraid—of not knowing what will happen or how it'll all work out."

"And being afraid of the unknown isn't much of a reason to decide anything," I replied, finishing his thought. "We'd never be here right now if we thought that way."

"No," he smiled. "We wouldn't."

...

"The weather outside is frightful," Hig sang loudly, and out of tune. "That fire was so delightful... But we've got places to go... #%!@ the snow! #%!@ the snow! #%!@ the snow!"

Halfway up a thousand-foot pass above Windy Bay, thigh-deep in punchy snow, Hig decided to modify the familiar winter carol. Between the towns of Chignik and Perryville, the coastline was steep and crenulated—more cliffs than beach. Each day we woke hoping to packraft around it, and each day the weather pushed us into the passes behind the headlands.

My foot sank into Hig's track, and snow caved in around it. I scrabbled with my soggy mittened hands to free my shoe from where it was cemented into the slope. Sheets of snow blew up the mountain behind us. I stood on a slushy avalanche pile, watching wet fat snowflakes streak past the whipping tops of the bushes, whiting out the world beyond. The snow came thicker and faster, accumulating on us and our gear, on the old snow, on the budding alder branches, and on the newly sprouted pushki greens.

It was May 22. It was the heaviest snow we'd seen all year. I couldn't decide whether to be amused or in total despair.

We dropped down toward sea level, following a large set of bear tracks to a trail through the alder. The snow turned to sleet, and the gusts only came harder, bending patches of thigh-thick alder down with each gust. Even in our jaded view as windswept explorers, this wind was howling. This wind was roaring. This was a storm to be reckoned with. Who knew how fast it blew? We didn't carry any instrument that could measure its speed, but we knew it was time for us to start hiding. Perhaps we would have minded less in shiny new dry suits. But the gale-force sleet drove into all the tiny fire holes, leaky seams, and worn-out patches in the dry suits we had been wearing since Anchorage.

In eleven and a half months of travel, we had become connoisseurs of wind. Wind that sweeps up from behind, shoving us along. Wind that drives in from ahead, stinging our exposed cheeks and noses. Wind that rattles the brush and flattens the grass. Wind that sets the water into a frothing chop. Wind that sends swirls of hissing snow streaming across the ground. Wind that blows for days, as if you'll never hear silence again. Wind that leaps up in an instant, bringing a roaring tempest that ends as suddenly as it began. Wind that blows sand, or snow, or leaves, or rain, or nothing at all. Wind that funnels through narrow notches in the land, where you can walk from a gale to dead calm in a matter of minutes. Wind that seems to fill the whole world.

. . .

Whooof! Slaaap! The yellow and grey walls of our pyramid flapped sharply inwards at every gust, spraying drops on the dry bags we'd used to barricade the edges of our bed. Hiding behind silnylon walls in a scrubby patch of alders, we listened to the hissing, spattering, and splashing sounds as the snow turned to sleet, to hail, to rain, and back again. Each form of precipitation was lobbed at our walls with a deafening violence.

The clothes and sleeping bags we huddled in had kept us warm in weather fifty degrees colder, but I still shivered, evaporating the water from my sodden clothes. As the wind whipped the alders, even their roots shook, sending vibrations under our bed. A small earthquake rocked our camp. We felt the shaking, but knew nothing of the quake until we reached the next village. In the violence of the storm, we couldn't tell the earthquake from the wind.

We huddled in our shelter against the roaring night. Our clothes and bed slowly dried to a cozy warmth. The next morning we listened to the alders thrash. Just beyond our thin walls was a world that would soak us, batter us, and blow us off our feet. We decided to wait out the storm.

It was the end of May, and the end of a long cold Alaska winter spent nearly completely outdoors. One day our world was green and bursting with life and birdsong. The next day it was harsh and bound by wind and snow. We celebrated every sprout. We cursed every snowflake. That morning, we made a decision. It was time for new life—not just for the snow-battered landscape, but for ourselves. It was time for a family.

16. VOLCANIC SHORES

Erin: I wondered when the last time was that
we'd been naked in the light of day.

WEARING WINTER HATS on their summer vacation, Perryville's children climbed in the alder shrubs, staring at us each time we walked past. We walked up and down a street lined by identical blue and brown houses, sending every dog in the village into an eruption of noisy barking. I nervously looked down at my feet, unusually conscious of how strange we must look—two white faces with two lumpy backpacks, bodies clothed in tattered dry suits. We didn't know anyone in this village. They didn't know we were coming. I imagine the children thought the circus had come to town.

Perryville was founded by refugees from the 1912 eruption of Katmai volcano farther up the coast. The present-day town perches beneath the towering hulk of the snow-capped Veniaminoff volcano—tempting the same fate. Scattered clusters of houses are tucked into a plain of alders, framed by grassy hills, steep cliffy headlands, and a smooth beach of black volcanic sand.

Veniaminoff crumbles, building the long beaches of glistening black sand farther and farther out to sea, leaving the spires of former islands stranded in fields of grass. A warming climate sends new plants and animals marching across the land. Fifty years ago, there wasn't a shrub in the village.

Two volcanoes, Pavlof and Pavlof Sister, tower over a rock-strewn lagoon on the Alaska Peninsula's Pacific coast.

Now brushy alders and grass creep over lands where tundra and berries once grew. Fifty years ago, folks living here had never seen a moose. Now these giant shrub-eaters are commonly hunted, while the tundra-loving caribou are becoming a more rare sight.

We stayed with Chief Gerald and his family at the Oceanside Estates, in one of the identical houses near the end of the row. Not that anyone called the subdivision by such a grandiose name. As in other villages, the development was known as "Hudville"—government-subsidized housing constructed by the U.S. Department of Housing and Urban Development.

A small digital readout on the kitchen wall showed how much credit remained on the pre-paid electric bill. When the credit runs out, off go the lights. The village generator ran on barged-in diesel, and as fuel prices skyrocketed, folks were wondering how they'd afford to power the town at all. The town had windmills, but they were still in boxes, waiting as the village tribe struggled to navigate the complex paperwork required for setting them up legally. The elaborate rules designed to protect birds from the whirling blades seemed out of place in this landscape where people were a tiny speck in a great wilderness.

A flat screen TV dominated the living room, on nearly every minute of the day. When Gerald's two kids were done examining every piece of our hiking gear, they fell asleep on the couch in front of the TV—this night and every night.

When we talked to the locals about fishing, hunting, and gathering, their eyes lit up. They gave us tips about the best way to cook young pushki and how to eat chitons from the rocks. But dinner came from a shelf of processed foods—white rice, canned corn, and canned sausages. We were grateful for their generosity in sharing their meal, but we wondered what dinner would have been a few decades ago. Folks here seemed to know all about the surrounding terrain, but most rarely went out in it.

It was a contradiction we had found in nearly every native village. People struggled to balance ancient traditions with modern lifestyles, in a place where either one is a very difficult way to live.

. . .

As we walked the beach in the morning, a wave sloshed onto the gravel, and I dipped my toes in the Pacific Ocean. In the evening, this time on purpose, I dipped my toes into the Bering Sea. The peninsula was narrow now, just a fringe of land connecting a string of volcanoes. Soon, it would be only a few miles wide.

All winter long, our yellow rubber boats had been consigned to serving as sleds and ground cloths. But as spring sprung, the packrafts finally came back into their own. The cool clear waters of a gentle river carried us down from the flanks of Veniaminoff, where we paddled the shores of Stepovak Bay.

Low fog kissed the lush green of the rye grass that lined the black sand beaches. Seals followed the edge of the breaking surf, staring at us with their inscrutable smooth faces. Puffins bobbed in the waves. The rock walls of lava dikes protruded into the sea like the fortifications of a long-gone castle. Waterfalls poured from cliffs of columnar basalt, painting them green with stripes of moss. The moist and chilly breeze gently nudged us along. A bear walking the beach ran as we paddled by, his muscles rippling under his dark brown fur as he charged up the steep grassy slope.

We rolled up the boats, heading over the pass. We followed a caribou. Skinny and alone, he trotted downstream ahead of us on the braided river plain, leaving a line of hoof prints in scattered patches of sand, darting between corpses of flood-tossed alders. There wasn't a patch of tundra or a piece of lichen in sight. I wondered what he was eating.

Caribou had been scarce this journey. We'd seen them only a handful of times, with the largest group composed of only a couple dozen animals. It appeared that the Alaska Peninsula's caribou were in trouble, and people we talked to in the villages confirmed our hunch. All three of the herds from here to Unimak were in a steep decline, for reasons no one quite understood. A heavy load of parasites and disease had been found in some of the animals. Other suspects included insufficient copper and selenium in their diet, and predation by bears and wolves. State wildlife biologists had turned to drastic measures—shooting wolves from helicopters and killing wolf cubs in their dens to try and shift the numbers.

The caribou we'd been watching eventually wandered off toward the edge of the valley, browsing on grass while he let us pass by.

The stream he led us down was small, unnamed, and braided into a handful of channels. But it was full, pulsing with high water. We shot through the valley in our packrafts, wobbling across eddy lines as we fought to stay in the deepest water, weaving between the channels as they split and joined. Before we knew it, we were spit out into the Bering Sea, bobbing in calm green-brown water and surrounded by a flotilla of curious sea otters. They nearly tipped over as we approached, leaning far out of the water to get a good look, before surrendering their nice dry paws and diving in retreat.

• • •

Cresting the beach berm at the Port Moller hot springs, we were greeted by curls of steam rising from a tiny trickle. The narrow strip of warmth was surrounded by a profusion of bright yellow monkey flowers and the most luscious greenery we'd seen all spring. A weathered cabin sat above the rock-lined pool. Most of its windows were gone, but someone had left several towels hanging on a hook beside the door. Near-boiling water bubbled from a small pool of mineral-coated sand, cooling as it wound its way down to the bathing pool. This oasis of warmth had drawn people since long before the fishermen who now frequented the site. The clamshell middens that lined the winding trails were covered by scattered beer cans, being slowly grown over by the tundra in their turn.

We slipped in to the rock-lined bathing pool, stirring up clouds of brown algae with our toes. The refraction of sunlight through the water turned the edges of clamshell fragments on the bottom into rainbows. We lounged in luxurious warmth, never even noticing our shoulders getting sunburned. I wondered when the last time was that we'd been naked in the light of day.

And I wondered how ancient this manmade pool really was. Who were the first people to discover the steaming trickle? How long ago did they dig the first pool? Free hot water must have been an even more important resource to ancient villagers than to lazy adventurers.

· · ·

The clock ticked away. We had two timelines to watch now. One was the "food clock" we had on every leg, spurring us onward with the threat of hunger. But now, for the first time in nearly a year, we also had a schedule with dates and times and numbers. On June 29, at 7 AM, we planned to be boarding a ferry from False Pass to Seldovia, and one way or another, the trip would have to be finished by then. But the water was perfect. And despite the fact that we'd been traveling for almost a year—maybe because of it—we needed a vacation.

Peering over the lip of our pool, I saw the ocean had disappeared—low tide turning the waters we'd rafted into a vast sand flat. Inspired by the middens and the shell-covered sand, we set out, shovel-less and bucket-less, to try and dig some clams.

We wandered to the edge of the open sand flats and started digging random holes between the rocks with the end of a paddle blade, pulling out a few tiny cockles. I had never gone clamming before and quickly realized that what I knew (that you went out on the tide flats with a shovel) didn't actually tell me anything about how to *find* the clams.

Farther out on the miles of sand flats, we began to look for holes, scrabbling in the dark, muddy sand with our bare hands. Unfortunately, many things that are not clams make holes in the sand. Especially worms. We unearthed several handfuls of these, along with some clams that were roughly the size of a quarter, and one half-crushed razor clam.

But that razor clam gave us hope. There was something to find here, if we could ever figure it out. Even farther from shore now, we continued to look for holes. With each handful of dark sandy goo, my knowledge leaped forward. The holes had different sizes, different shapes, and some of them—the ones that were a little oblong, a little deep—housed razor clams! Plunging my hands into the sand, I tried to outrace the clams, pinching them between my fingers as I dug, working not to crush their fragile shells. Razor clams accumulated in a nylon bag. Our cook pot was tiny, but all thoughts of limiting our harvest quickly flew from my mind. We were finding food!

My hands were rubbed raw. Sand filled the space under my fingernails until it seemed like the sheer volume of grit might pry them off. The tide was coming in. But the joy of gathering food had turned me obsessive. I couldn't stop digging.

A hundred yards ahead of me, Hig was already walking back to shore, carrying the clams in our muddy orange inflation bag. "Come on! We're getting flooded in!"

"I'm coming!"

I took a few running footsteps shoreward, splashing through the rising water. Then I stopped dead in my tracks, muddy fingers plunging back into the sand. "Just one more!"

There were several more. Our cook pot stuffed to bursting, we steamed the clams in Port Moller's hottest bubbling pool. Farther down, in more habitable water, we feasted. I plucked razor clams out of their shells, dipping them in a pot lid full of butter. Each one exploded lusciously in my mouth. The second potful became a rich, buttery chowder, stuffed with a half dozen different species of wild greens gathered from the edges of the stream. As the day slowly waned, we made no move to pack up—walking could wait.

• • •

At Port Moller, it was spring. Less than a week later, on the flanks of Mount Dans it was winter again. Fluffy snowflakes the size of quarters drifted from the sky, settling on pussy willows and the sprouting tips of fireweed and pushki. They flew around in the breeze like torn bits of paper, dusting the mountains powdered-sugar white.

"This snow is actually kind of pretty," I commented, examining the delicate white flakes on the black sleeve of my dry suit.

We packed up, stomping our cold feet. It was June 5—and snowing. All I could do was laugh.

The wind came up from the southwest, picking up the snow in a whirling gale, battering our faces. It turned from snow, to sleet, and finally settled in on a driving rain. As the wet drops drove through our threadbare clothes, the wind only grew. We walked the infinite sands of Long Beach beneath Pavlof volcano, watching the grass whipping and storm waves frothing.

I kept my eyes on the ground, shielding them from the sting of the rain. Little shorebirds ran along the beach ahead of me, pecking at sand and kelp. I felt sorry for them—the wet sand blowing along the beach must be right in their eyes.

I had run out of patience with wind howling in my face. It felt like the world was yelling at us.

Hig rudely uprooted a scrawny willow. Its trunk was only as thick as my thin wrist, but in this climate, it might have been an ancient. I broke off a branch of another. The scrubby trees were only waist-high. We were clearing out a little space for our sleeping bag in this tiny patch of shrubbery. The willows grew here because of the slight lee provided by a small hill. They damped the wind, just a little, as it galloped over the hilltop.

Most of the willows shared our tent with us. It was early in the afternoon, but too wet and miserable to travel farther. And who knew where we might find another patch of willows?

I slept fitfully. In Perryville, we had mailed our down quilt from Perryville to Seldovia and were now left with just our "summer" bag. Even though we'd slept through much colder nights with this same bag, I missed the luxurious warmth of the quilt. Perhaps, as we approached the end of the journey, I could more easily imagine the comfort of not being outside in every storm.

We were approaching the Aleutian Islands. I thought of how other authors had titled the Aleutians. Corey Ford called them "Where the Sea Breaks Its Back." Bernard Hubbard had called it the "Cradle of the Storms."

Cold air sweeps down the Bering Sea from the Arctic. Warm air sweeps up from the Pacific. High pressure and low-pressure zones break over this skinny ridge of volcanoes, birthing swirling storms. From here, they sweep along the Gulf of Alaska, battering the rest of the Pacific coast. The storms that pummeled us on the Lost Coast were all born here. On the very end of the Alaska Peninsula, folks at the Cold Bay weather station wrestle with weather balloons to launch them in fifty-knot gales, providing data on the storms before they hit the rest of the country. This is where the weather comes from.

...

A plume of steam rose from a jagged bite in a round white cone. A fortress of lava columns stood against the sky, like a castle from a fantastical world. Where the storms are born, the land is also new, erupted from the depths of the earth. Lava ridges and cinder plains flanked snow-topped cones. Every pebble and grain on the beach was formed of bubbly red and black lava. Pavlof and Pavlof Sister—perfect rounded cones reaching eight thousand feet above the landscape—towered over everything.

Thirteen hundred feet above the beach, twisting fins of black lava knifed above the snow, pockmarked, crenellated, and viciously sharp. June's hot sun beamed on the snow slopes, melting them into a mush we sank knee-deep into with every step. Bear tracks marked the snow everywhere—some traversing the landscape in purposeful lines, while the tracks of the cubs left weaving figure eights as they played. We saw bears nearly every day now, but I was surprised to find them in a such a barren environment.

I buried my mouth in our bag of Grape Nuts. Perryville had been a difficult place to resupply, and we didn't have much food left that I could stomach. I knew I would only be making it even worse for the remaining few days, but I couldn't quite bring myself to dive back into our tubs of canned frosting. Hig was kicking up a wall of snow around the edges of our shelter. My toes were already cold from climbing through the wet summer snow, and they ached a little more just watching him. But I climbed off the lava spire to come help anyway. Even under the calm evening sunshine, we prepared for wind.

...

Days, then weeks, then months had slipped by. And when June 9, 2008 arrived, we felt we needed to do something to celebrate. It was the one-year anniversary of the start of our trip.

Three hundred and sixty-six days since we'd left Seattle (it was a leap year), we packed up our camp with a series of calm and practiced steps, reminiscing about the chaos of June 9, 2007. On that morning, a crowd of friends and family had joined us in the heart of our busy urban neighborhood. This time, we had only the birds and the bears for companionship.

With the exception of our parents, we hadn't seen any of those people in a year. The list of things we hadn't done in a year—hanging out with friends, traveling in a motorized vehicle, wearing our own ordinary clothing—spanned nearly everything normal. But the list of things we had done and seen in the past year was simply extraordinary.

At the beginning of our trip, my brain had been full of intense and swirling emotions—exhaustion from all our preparations, relief at finally beginning, excitement about what was to come, and trepidation about what we were getting into.

Now, as we stopped for a celebratory meal of spaghetti, beans, and fresh spring greens on the gravel banks of the Joshua Green River, I tried to determine how I felt.

I felt a little hungry—nothing unusual. I felt eager to see the next place we were heading for—Izembek Lagoon. Mostly, I just felt comfortable. I didn't feel anything particularly "momentous" about this momentous anniversary. I had expected this day would feel like a milestone—something to congratulate ourselves on. Instead, it was just a normal day. Which is to say, extraordinary.

Each of our days was characterized by something extraordinary. This day it was a tense encounter with a golden-brown bear and Hig's discovery of a large, rare glass ball on the coast of the Bering Sea. The day before, it had been difficult navigation along a snowy caldera rim in a whiteout of fog. Before that, it had been following winding bear trails over alder- and tundra-covered lava. And before that, it had been a day stretching our legs in long strides along open beaches, listening to the cries of arctic terns overhead. Each day had its own unforgettable story. And today was another ordinary extraordinary day. Our journey could be considered "extreme" in all sorts of ways. But at this point, it was, quite simply, our everyday life.

· · ·

We'd been warned about False Pass for a long time, and had been worrying about it for even longer. It was only a mile across—barely a half hour's paddle. But we'd walked enough of the Alaska Peninsula to expect a nearly constant wind and to be wary of storms. And in this crossing, we also had to worry about the tides.

False Pass is a narrow channel at the very end of the Alaska Peninsula—connecting the Pacific Ocean and Bering Sea for the very first time. Different tides on the two seas send strong currents whipping through the passage—unpredictable with our bare-bones tide tables. Everyone said the currents were wild and dangerous.

We had a lot of experience with tides, and that only intensified my concern. I conjured up a mental "worst-case" amalgam of all that I've seen tides do: monster whirlpools, standing waves, slack tides that last less than a minute... Add in chaotic swells and the wild and unpredictable winds of the Alaska Peninsula, and I didn't know what we were in for. Our only saving grace was that a crossing in June couldn't be complicated by ice.

Our plan was solid. We'd sit at the narrow point, watching the currents to see how they shifted and swirled—waiting for a gap in the weather. All we needed was a half hour window, and we'd planned for at least an extra day.

But it kept nagging at my mind. It wasn't the end of the journey, but the one mile of water at False Pass was the final obstacle standing between us and the Aleutian Islands. We'd been telling people we were headed to these mythical islands for over a year now. What if, here at the very end, we couldn't do it?

. . .

When we finally reached False Pass, slight ripples of current marred the smooth surface of the dark-blue water. Red-painted cannery buildings rose up on the other side of the narrow channel—almost glowing in the patchy sunlight. Sea ducks sat on the kelp, which was stretched out in a gentle current. There wasn't a whirlpool or whitecap in sight. We hardly paused before inflating our boats and launching.

As we closed in on the last hundred yards of smooth water between us and the Aleutians, I turned to Hig with a grin. "I don't see a 'death scenario' here."

"I don't even see an 'inconvenient walk into town' scenario," Hig replied.

The last major obstacle of the journey flew beneath our paddles in twenty easy minutes. Or at least, the last major obstacle we'd been expecting.

17. VICTORY LAP

Erin: "We don't have enough thread!"

IT WAS MIDNIGHT in False Pass. I had borrowed our host's computer, sitting alone in a darkened room for a late night Googling of my symptoms, confirming my suspicions.

"Hig," I whispered, as I crawled in to join him in our sleeping bag on the floor, "I really think I'm pregnant."

"Wow." There was a few seconds pause, both of us staring at each other. "Are you sure?"

"Not completely, not without a test. But I'm pretty sure. Are we ready for this?" I asked nervously.

Hig reached over, squeezing my shoulder. "Well, I guess we are."

I smiled. I was excited for this child. But in hindsight, I had to wonder about the wisdom of carrying him or her along for the last 500 miles of a harsh and difficult expedition. I'd been taking vitamins and eating lots of spring greens, but also lots of junk food—cans of frosting sprang to mind. And we'd been short of food walking into Cold Bay. We were often short of food. What could that do to a growing baby?

"Hig, if we run short of food on this leg…Well, I think I should eat enough to replenish what I'm burning. So you might end up more hungry…."

"I know. It's OK," he reassured me.

Erin peers out from a cocoon of mist-drenched clothing during one of Unimak Island's wet and windy storms.

. . .

When we walked out of False Pass, we were four. Hig and I, the unborn child I was carrying, and Eric. We'd become friends with Eric in Anchorage, crashing in his apartment in between attempts to negotiate Knik Arm. Eric runs a tiny biking gear company, and we bonded with him over packrafting, sewing talk, and scraps of nylon. Eric is also a filmmaker. He'd already put together several short videos on our trip from some of our footage, and was planning to make a whole movie about the journey.

He wanted to join us for a section of the trip. Throughout the past year, it had never worked, logistically or otherwise, for someone to join us for more than a couple days. This sounded like fun.

But a good part of my mind had already reached the end of the journey—straying toward the future, wondering about our life beyond, our unborn child. We had already reached the Aleutians, and this last leg seemed almost an afterthought. The plan was to make it as far as we could—not only to reach Unimak Island—but to reach the island's farthest tip, then circle back to the town of False Pass. I was committed to the idea, set down before we even left Seattle. But was it simply a technicality? After walking the entire Alaska Peninsula—after walking for 373 days—a "victory lap" seemed silly.

. . .

But even after 4,000 miles, there's always more to see. The last scrubby bushes gave way to sweeping fields of tundra, grass, and broken lava. At a ragged headland, we blew up the packrafts and took to the sea. Three little boats bobbed up and down in a several-foot swell, water rushing up to obscure our horizon. Hig and Eric each held a video camera, leapfrogging back and forth along the shore to film each other. Steep cliffs faded into grey mists above us, dizzying in their height. Dikes of lava built strange spires and pinnacles, molding themselves into walls, knife-like ridges, and hidden caves. Seagulls wheeled and screamed around us, the pungent scent of their guano surrounding every sea stack. A golden-blond bear napped on a grassy cliff-top knoll. A pair of eagles nested on a fifty-foot rock, squeaking their agitation.

Back on shore, clouds of mist blew along the black sand ripples, leaving jewel-like drops of condensation on the worn fibers of our dry suits and the new shoots of rye grass. Fog crept across the camera lenses and hovered over the sea. We spent a day beneath the flanks of an imposing nine-thousand-foot volcano, but saw it only on the map. In our view, there was nothing more than the soft green of grassy dunes, the black of volcanic sand, and the grey of ocean and sky.

The air sat calmly on the land. Fog pressed down on the world, softening and slowing its mood. Surf crashed. An abandoned fishing boat testified to the risks of this angry sea; all but the wheelhouse sunk in a sea of sand waves. Breaking waves and drifting mist painted shifting patterns of white against the static pattern of black sand ripples. They mesmerized me. The three of us walked along silently, each absorbed in our separate thoughts.

· · ·

"Guys, I think we have a problem."

Hig and I scrambled up from our seats around the fire, hurrying to follow Eric up the small rise that separated our fire on the beach from our tent on the grass. I couldn't see what Eric saw, but on Unimak Island—a place where the nine hundred bears vastly outnumber the sixty or so people—I could guess what a "problem" was likely to be.

I crested the dune, just in time to see a big sassy brown bear ambling away from where our tent had stood moments before. We'd left everything ready—a perfectly set-up pyramid shelter, taut and square with every tie tied out, cozy beds laid out inside, and our gear arranged around them. We'd only been a hundred yards away, cooking dinner on the beach. And suddenly, everything was gone.

I slowly walked over to the remains of our camp, not sure if I wanted to see.

"We don't have enough thread!"

I stared down at the tattered mess that minutes before had been our home. The bear had managed to slash holes in nearly every panel of our pyramid shelter. It had punctured all three sleeping pads, gleefully shredding one into at least a dozen tiny pieces. One packraft was torn open.

Several dry bags were bitten through. My passport and Hig's credit card were stamped with tooth marks. The bear's foot had cracked a paddle blade. About the only thing it hadn't destroyed was our food, settling for one big bite out of a stack of tortillas and a bag of mangoes.

After hundreds of nights camping in bear country—often sleeping with our food in the tent—this was the first time a bear had bothered our camp. And it didn't even want the food.

I realized what we'd done wrong. Instead of choosing a campsite away from bear travel corridors as we usually did, we'd set up camp barely a stone's throw from the beach and right on the banks of a little stream—right where a bear might walk.

It was at least a three days' walk back to False Pass, the nearest town. It was midnight. And just then, it started to rain.

The bright lights of anchored fishing boats shone offshore, and we briefly considered paddling out in one of the packrafts to ask for aid.

"What are we going to ask them for?" Eric wondered "Thread?"

"A tarp," Hig answered. "But let's first see what we can repair."

I was tired. All I wanted to do was to go home. But our home was shredded. I stared sadly at its remains, wondering if it was even possible to make it functional again. It wasn't just a roof I wanted. After so many cozy nights, I really loved that pyramid shelter. I loved the packraft the bear had bitten through. Our gear had brought us through so much. Leaving it up on the tundra for the bear to get, I felt a strange sense of guilt at having failed it.

We gathered up handfuls of our battered possessions, and retreated to our fire on the beach. I stretched out behind a log, pulling a deflated pack-raft over me—a too-small roof. A steady stream of water ran onto and under my head, leaving my hood and hair completely sodden. I carved out a little hollow for my hip, but the sand was hard. Eric was curled up somewhere nearby. I slept cold and fitfully. Hig gamely took the first shift, working by the fire under the beam of our only headlamp, listening for the bear, his sewing needle pulling the shorn fabric together.

It was the middle of June, when darkness barely skimmed the land. By the time Hig woke Eric for the second shift, daylight had returned. When I finally woke, I felt grumpy and disheartened. I didn't *want* to be resilient and adaptable. I didn't *want* to deal with yet another obstacle. We had only eight days left of this journey. We'd come so far already. We had dealt with so much ....

But by then, the shelter was no longer a heap of shreds. Two walls were mostly intact, and the main structural lines were repaired so it stood—a battered but familiar shape. Our situation was already starting to improve.

By ten in the morning, we had three pairs of busy hands, needles flying along bear-claw gashes, slowly whipstitching fraying tears into tough new scar tissue. I sat cross-legged in one corner of the shelter, sewing hole after hole. Eric lay on his back on the other side, working from the inside out. Hig was by the fire again, carefully repairing the packraft with a flawless baseball stitch. My confidence had returned. We could manage this, the way we'd managed blizzards and thin ice, bone-chilling cold and short rations, missing maps and howling wind, torn boots and broken ski poles. The rain had stopped, and drying sand sloughed off our clothing in clumps. Slowly, amazingly, our gear began to take shape.

In the end, it took the rest of our dental floss, thirty-one combined hours of labor, and one-third of a tube of waterproof glue. Altogether, we had mended almost thirty feet of tears, including two feet on the sleeping pads, two feet on a raft, one foot-long crack on a paddle blade, and over twenty-four feet on our shelter. Everything we owned looked like the Frankenstein's monster version of hiking gear. One of the sleeping pads was completely unsalvageable. Some of the dry bags we didn't even bother with. But we could sleep dry, and we could paddle without sinking. By seven the next night, we were on our way again.

• • •

We walked on with the dawning realization that we had solved one problem only to run into another: We didn't have enough food.

Packing up to leave "bad bear camp," I piled all our bags of food next to a log, sorting them into each of our dry bags. I hadn't taken a good look at our food since we'd packed it in False Pass. It looked small. Awfully small.

My rough guess put it at thirty pounds—five days of food when we ought to have had seven.

Had the bear taken more than we'd realized? Did Eric really eat that much more than Hig and I? Or had we all been eating more than usual—tempted by the availability of two cook pots and a selection of food better than our normal fare? Perhaps we had miscalculated back in False Pass? It didn't matter. We didn't have enough food, and losing a day to repairs had only made it worse. And this time, I worried what hunger might do to the child growing inside me. It didn't seem fair, but Eric and Hig would have to bear the brunt of the discomfort.

Hunger is a rare thing in our wealthy American world. But on this journey, hunger had become a frequent and familiar companion. To chink the gaps in our rations, we had raided lodges for mountain house meals and packets of cocoa. We had received gifts of everything from fresh crab meat to stale trail mix—from fishermen, sailors, hunters, homesteaders, and mining camp workers in out of the way places. We'd even grabbed two-year-old Wheat Thins and spaghetti from the moldy logging trailers at Surf Inlet.

And we had gathered what we could. In the summer, we had picked berries. In the fall, we ate mushrooms. And now spring had covered the ground with a profusion of edible life. But when you're focused on calories, plants are just garnish. All the wonderful spring greens we could gather added flavor and vitamins but few calories to our meager meals.

We carefully rationed the remaining food: one bag of "Buttery Goodness" and a bit of pasta to get us through Fisher Caldera, another few meager ziplocs of rice, beans, and cheese for another piece of terrain, and a last meal of mashed potatoes and a few gulps of lemonade to get us home.

. . .

Eric's feet scrabbled on the empty window frame, disappearing onto the roof. I followed, careful to avoid the broken glass and nails littering the moldering ruin. We stood on the roof of the second Scotch Cap lighthouse, built to replace the one that had been destroyed when a tsunami swept this coast in 1946. In the decades since, the newer structure had fallen into disrepair, abandoned in favor of a tiny battery-powered and computer-run light. The site of the first lighthouse was nothing more than a mangled foundation, where knots of twisted rebar protruded from the tatters of a few concrete walls. The Coast Guard men who had manned the lighthouse died in that wave, and a bronze plaque memorializing them had been erected in the second structure.

Bluish smudges of land appeared on the southwestern horizon—the next few islands in the Aleutian chain. Huge container ships cruised past, heading back and forth to Asia. The Aleutians were only beginning. But for us, it was the end of the line.

We walked beyond the lighthouse remains, munching fistfuls of succulent sweet beach greens and gathering stray sticks of firewood. And when we reached the southwestern-most point of land—the very tip of Unimak Island—we stopped for a celebratory lunch of rice and beans.

Unimak Island is the outer limit of the bear's range, the outer limit of the caribou's range, and the outer limit of the packrafter's range. Twelve treacherous miles of Unimak Pass stood between us and the next island's shore. Strong currents, huge container ships, and the Aleutians' ever-present winds only added to the danger. There had been no question since we'd first started planning this expedition. We would go no farther west.

As hungry as we were, it was easy to swoon over the celebratory lunch. But no one was standing on the beach with champagne, clapping us on the back for a job well done. And Scotch Cap was never really our goal. It was just an unremarkable wiggle in the coastline—a plain gravel beach with tufts of sprouting beach greens and one screaming eagle, defending its sea stack nest. We were still in the middle of nowhere, still short of food, and still five days from the nearest town. Just like our one-year anniversary, it was another ordinary extraordinary day, unforgettable for its unique adventures, but unremarkable when set beside the other days of our journey.

• • •

On the map, Unimak Island is dominated by the imposing presence of four major volcanoes. From the ground, we hardly saw them. Swirls of mist and fog draped our world, shrouding spires and columns of volcanic rock in a blanket of moody grey. Solstice had come and gone, and with it our fifth wedding anniversary—the second one we'd celebrated in the course of this journey. Summer had officially arrived. And along with the blooming flowers and budding leaves, summer had turned our snow to rain.

It had been a day in which the wind and rain seemed to be playing a cruel game—fighting to see which would come out the strongest. It was the windiest rain and the rainiest wind. Packrafting had left us sitting in pools of water, in an atmosphere that was almost a pool of water itself. We were sodden through each and every layer of clothing—swimming in our skins.

We looked for a suitable camp spot. Out on this farthest tip of Unimak Island, there wasn't even a waist-high bush to hide behind.

. . .

When we first glimpsed the White Alice site, it was impossible to tell how far away it was. Giant boxy towers and huge radar dishes peered out through the mists, perched on a barren ridge in the middle of nowhere, spooky in their hulking abandonment. To us, they meant only one thing—the possibility of walls and a roof.

No one I talked to could ever tell me where the name "White Alice" came from. This site once boasted state-of-the-art communications technology, until satellites made it obsolete. In the past, signals had bounced from giant radar dish to giant radar dish, sending messages between stations strung across the far corners of Alaska.

Pools of greasy water glistened on the floor. Doors were torn off their hinges by past storms, and hulking vacuum-tube computers rusted in shadowed rooms. The moldering building stank of gasoline. Pregnancy had heightened my sense of smell, and I could barely tolerate the stench. Eric really wanted the shelter of those walls. I huddled outside, slumped against the building, waiting to see if Hig would come up with some acceptable compromise.

. . .

Quarter-sized flecks of paint peeled from the walls, piling on the floor like beige confetti. We perched on a landing of a fifth-floor stairwell, feeding old doors and planks into the roaring blaze we'd built on a metal plate. This high in the building, the puddles and smell were gone. But even inside four walls, the wind rushed around us, damp and chilly.

Hig balanced a piece of plywood on his hand, and brought it up toward the open hatch above our fire. Two feet short of the opening, the wind grabbed it, hurling it straight up so it vanished into the rushing mists. When we'd finished using our fire, we pitched the coals and smoldering planks upward through the hole—into the rainstorm.

When we'd dried off as much as we could, and eaten as much as we dared, I switched off my headlamp, plunging us into a darkness far more complete than we ever see outdoors in an Alaskan summer. Hig and I curled tightly together on our upside-down packrafts, warding off the chill.

Our "dismal fortress" didn't just creak in the wind. It shrieked like a banshee. It howled and crashed, clanked and groaned and thrummed, throbbed and knocked. It pounded as if a entire company of ghostly soldiers was sprinting up the stairs to kick us out—bitter at having been left to station such a bleak and angry corner of the world.

· · ·

The tide washed the bears' tracks away. The bears left more, clustering around a slab of rotting whale blubber. We walked in their footsteps as we retraced our own, back to False Pass along the southern coast of Unimak Island. When the beaches disappeared, we followed their trails up onto the tundra, walking a worn dirt path between new flowers and crumbling lava.

Rounding a corner on the trail, we nearly stumbled into a bear. He stood up slowly, sniffing our scent, taking a few steps on his hind legs like a wobbly circus bear. No interest in messing with a trio of hikers, the resigned look in his eyes said. "This is *my* trail. Why do *I* have to go around?" He was brown bear number twelve since we'd left False Pass—twelve bears in only ten days. I tried to keep the three of us walking in a tight group—excited to see the bears, but hoping to make our little trio into a more imposing presence.

On another day, high on the tundra flanks of Westdahl volcano, we were circled by seven caribou, trotting circles around us with their graceful gait and goofy curiosity. On another evening, we were followed for half an hour by a cute and curious orange and black fox. And on all the days and nights, we listened to the calls of the birds, shifting along with each transition in the landscape.

Even in the short time between walking out to Scotch Cap and returning to False Pass, the world had taken several more leaps into summer. The twiggy grey branches of the alders exploded into bright green leaves and yellow tassels of pollen, covering everything with a yellow dust. Bright green springs burst from volcanic hillsides, flowing down into deeply cut gullies of grass and wildflowers.

The closer we got toward summer, the easier it was to see: for all its harsh weather, this part of the world is one of the most alive places I've ever been.

. . .

As we walked the last few beaches separating us from civilization, Hig and I discussed baby names, quickly agreeing that the child would have to bear the name of an Alaskan volcano.

We packed up from our last night of camping, just like every other night. We tramped into False Pass, gorging ourselves on food and searching for a roof for the night, as we had done in so many villages before. Over the course of a year, we had walked, paddled, and skied 4,171 miles. The incomprehensibly long trip was over, but that fact hadn't sunk in yet.

It was the end of our world. I couldn't decide whether to be excited about the new world stretching before us, or nostalgic for the one we were leaving. We had made so many plans during our long walk. Now that we had accomplished one extravagant goal we'd set for ourselves, we had to start looking toward the next. Not all of our days could be extraordinary. But our lives still could be.

"Hey, Hig. Let's do this same trip again, in twenty-five years. It'll be enough time to see how things have changed, but soon enough that we can probably still pull it off."

Hig grinned. "Actually, I think that's a really good idea."

Epilogue: FINDING HOME

"ARE YOU GOING to walk back?"

It was a question we'd been asked almost from the beginning of our journey. At first we laughed, assuming the question must be in jest. But after the hundredth time I heard it, I started to wonder. For over a year, we had been "the people who walked from Seattle." Our journey defined our identity. So perhaps it was natural to assume that when the journey ended, the walkers would turn around and walk back home, rewinding the whole process until they were swallowed back into whatever normal life they'd come from.

But long before we reached Unimak Island, we knew we weren't going back. We hadn't kept a house or apartment in Seattle. We'd given away most of our possessions. In remote cabin guest books and sign-in sheets—anywhere we were asked to fill in an address—we simply filled in the name of wherever we were standing. We lived anywhere and everywhere. But after a year as nomads, we were ready to start digging in.

Even in the midst of an expedition, Hig and I talk about future adventures. Some of them are plans for other journeys—swaths of country we wished we had time to see, or longed to return to. But on this trip, some of our discussions concerned plans for life. In a journey of 385 days, there are 9,240 hours. Even with the hours of sleep and the hours of silence, it's a lot of time for two people to talk about the future.

Sometime in the fall, we'd decided to stay in Alaska. Sometime in the winter, we'd decided to settle somewhere rural. And sometime in the spring, we had decided to come to Seldovia.

• • •

That summer, we built. Experts at tent pitching, both Hig and I were completely clueless about real construction. The more we worked, the more relieved I was that we weren't attempting a house—just a round platform for a yurt. Five little walls to hold our circular plywood floor up off the gravel slope.

Our half-built platform sat on a small corner of Hig's mother's land—occupying a narrow gap in a beautiful grove of spruce trees, butted up against a prolific old blueberry bush. We'd measured the entire placement of the yurt to avoid overrunning that bush, despite the extensive blueberry patch in the gully behind it. Every few days, I'd wander through with a pair of hedge clippers and a plastic yogurt container—pruning the evil devil's club away from my precious blueberries, and checking if any were ripe.

We were three miles outside of the center of town, on a winding gravel road. From our platform, we could look over the water and across to the mountains beyond. Our yard was a profusion of wild blueberries and salmonberries. A few steps from the platform, a trail climbed up into the alpine tundra. Another trail wound through the woods to a tiny lake, then to a rushing creek in a deep gorge. Beyond the ends of these short trails, wilderness beckoned.

Every weekend, we went to parties. Half the town appeared, each person toting a delicious dish, and many of them bringing instruments. We listened to live music, lounging outside in the long summer evenings as we learned to know our new neighbors. People brought us gifts—the wood to build our platform, the tools to put it together, firewood, a helping hand.

Here in Seldovia, we had wilderness. We had community. And we had family.

With a child soon to come, the presence of Hig's parents was the tipping point that led us here, choosing Seldovia over other small communities we had also loved. We fell easily into the routine of a pair of people playing at being settled—filling our freezer with berries and our canning jars with salmon, as we worked to set up our home.

. . .

It was nearly winter before we had a roof of our own. Fire blazed in our tiny woodstove, an orange glow shining through the smoky glass door. Outlets, shelves, and drying clothes hung from the fence-like wooden lattice that constitutes our walls. A curving pattern of red, yellow, and blue-painted stripes spiraled across our plywood floor. Beyond the rippled plastic of our windows, whitecaps roughened the surface of Cook Inlet far below. As winter extended into February, the sun returned from where it had hidden behind the mountains, touching down in a blaze of orange on the volcanoes across the inlet.

Our twenty-four foot yurt has been variously described as looking like a spaceship, an oil tank, and a hobbit hole. To us, it's the only home we've ever owned—the first time we've lived in a place that's really ours.

We live in a circle, 450 square feet of light and airy space, where the kitchen blends into the office blends into the bedroom blends into the woodpile in a comfortable chaos. When the west wind howls, our fabric walls flap in and out with every big gust. Glasses clink on the shelves, and the whole yurt shudders and rattles with the force of the storm. With each storm, I'm happy to be warm and comfortable, lightly dressed next to a crackling woodstove. But listening to the wind rage through our thin fabric house gives me a comforting connection to the world outside—almost as though we were still back in our thin nylon shelter.

. . .

A pair of people who've lived in the wild for a year must be at least a little bit feral—a little bit bearlike—a little bit wild. How could we seamlessly integrate into civilized society? Maybe living in a yurt, in a 300-person village beyond the end of the road system, doesn't count as civilized. We dip water from a primitive well and heat wash-water on the woodstove. Our sink drains into a pair of slop buckets, and our bathroom is an outhouse across the driveway. But here in our yurt, we have a microwave, an electric oven, laptop computers, and high-speed Internet. We also have piles of work that involve staring at a computer screen, shuffling paperwork, and managing a calendar with scheduled meetings and events. All of which sounds very "civilized."

Sometimes I do miss the simplicity of two people and two backpacks—with nothing to accomplish beyond one day's walk. Sometimes I'm grateful for the weatherproof yurt. Most of the time, I never even think about the difference. We loved our journey. But beyond the end of the expedition, we immersed ourselves in the tasks of settling as much as we'd immersed ourselves into our adventure. From the first step we took on that Seattle sidewalk, we never spent much time thinking about our old life. We stepped forward. And now, we've stepped forward again, into a different life. We may imagine future adventures, but we don't spend much time looking back.

• • •

The nurses told me I was the only person they'd ever heard of to walk half an hour up the hill to the hospital in the middle of active labor. Perhaps that was true. But unlike our journey, childbirth was an adventure billions had experienced before us.

I was surprised at how easily we slid into being parents. I didn't know much about babies—I don't think I'd ever changed a diaper. But when our son arrived, parenthood was just another transition. A transition like passing from summer calm to fall storms. Like a climb from beaches into mountains. Or like returning from the wilderness to civilization.

Our journey taught us to be good at transitions. To be adaptable. To embrace our immediate circumstances, and continue the journey under whatever those new conditions might be. We hadn't planned it as preparation for parenthood. But it was perfect.

• • •

Katmai Winter McKittrick. We named him for a volcano. On a clear day, our yurt has a view of three active volcanoes—Redoubt, Iliamna, and Augustine. It's a small slice of the mountain chain extending southwest down the Alaska Peninsula and out into the Aleutian Islands. Katmai's namesake is part of that chain, though it's not visible from our yurt. It lies a little farther south and west, sitting in the moonscape valley of hardened ash it produced in a massive 1912 eruption.

Mount Katmai is surrounded by Katmai National Park, a land of windswept tundra, convoluted fjords, and the edge of the spruce forests, populated by caribou and salmon-fed bears. It was a place we passed through and loved on our first expedition together, years before we'd ever thought of a child. It's a place we passed through on this journey and loved again, frozen and gleaming under an intense April sun.

Katmai went hiking the day he was conceived, hidden deep within my body. He journeyed over five hundred miles of wilderness before he was even born. Katmai went hiking the day he was born, as I headed up an icy hill to the hospital in the throes of labor. He went hiking the day after he was born, tucked in the wrap on Hig's chest as we walked back down the same hill. Nearly every day of his short existence, Katmai has gone hiking.

When he's old enough, we'll take him on an expedition to visit his namesake. But first we'll take him out to the Lost Coast. And then perhaps to the Northwest Arctic. Swirling plans in our adventure-addicted brains will keep us exploring. But along with all the new places, we'll rediscover all the wonders of our home—with the help of a new pair of eyes.

Acknowledgments

I'D LIKE TO THANK the long list of generous souls who helped us along the way, providing food, shelter, logistical help, and great company. They made this trip both more possible and a whole lot more enjoyable than it might have been without them. In roughly the order in which they helped us: Andrew, Shaun, Niki, John, Faith, Chris, Ted, Pat, Lela, Sue, Jill, Mike, Jobe, Kathy, Conny, John, Carol, Allie, Chris, Doug, Sunny, Bob, Marven, Nick, Neil, Lew, Rose, Gregory, Micah, Steph, Steve, Sylvia, Martha, Dave, Tim, Lee, Joseph, Eve, Beth, Donna, Phil, Bruce, One-Eyed Bob, Bob, Kathy, Kris, Howard, Bill, Tom, Jeff, Abby, Les, George, Jill, Jeff, Elizabeth, Tony, Neil, Tom, Brian, Don, Lahoma, Dixon, Cathy, Kelly, Paul, Janet, Kathy, Maggie, Amy, David, De, Nick, Robyn, Ralph, Eric, Roman, John, Phil, Dede, Monty, Karen, Randy, Judy, Larry, Kevin, Dennis, Steve, Ann, Bella, Lyle, Jaque, Dave, John, Leon, Angela, Charlotte, Trish, Vanessa, Margie, Carl, Gary, Todd, Jenny, Colter, Jeff, Dan, Josie, Mike, Courtney, Deanna, Missy, Mike, Priscilla, Ann, Cris, Jack, Doug, Viola, Carvel, Shirly, Hoss, April, Charles, Carol, Fred, Vic, Rollie, Mike, Wendy, Delissa, Heath, Gerald, Kristine, Aubrey, Sandra, Mike, Mark, countless other well-wishers, and anyone I might have forgotten!

I'd also like to thank the folks who helped me on the book—in alphabetical order: Andrew, David, Faith, Ingrid, Joan, Kate, and Tracy, and our sponsors: Alaska Conservation Foundation (Nick and Matt), Alpacka Raft (Andrew and Sheri), Backpacking Light (Carol, Ken, and Ryan), GoreTex (Shipton–Tilman Grant), Kedzig Innovation Group (John), Montrail Shoes (Paul), Mountain Laurel Designs (Ron), the Renewable Resources Coalition (Danny and Scott), SEAWEAD (Bob), Teko Socks, the Timmissartok Foundation, and Tom.

And finally, Hig and Katmai, who are an integral part of everything.

Erin and Katmai
ready for a hike in the snow

Erin McKittrick grew up in Seattle, exploring the nearby Cascade Mountains with her family. She met her husband, Hig, at Carleton College, from where she graduated in 2001 with a bachelor's degree in biology. That summer, the couple took off on their first major Alaskan adventure together, and haven't looked back since. Erin later earned a master's degree in molecular biology, but left academia to pursue writing. She also works as a photographer and as a jewelry manufacturer, and with her husband runs a small environmental non-profit called Ground Truth Trekking (www.GroundTruthTrekking.org). Erin and Hig use journeys like *A Long Trek Home* to explore the complexities of natural resource issues. They live with their son in Seldovia, Alaska, a 300-person village just beyond the reach of the road system.